Almost Our Time

Almost Our Time

Generation X Takes On America's Challenges

Rob Stam
with Greg Smith

This is a work of nonfiction. However, some names and details have been changed to respect privacy.

Cover design by Greg Smith of Black Lake Studio.

Published by Black Lake Press of Holland, Michigan.
Black Lake Press is a division of Black Lake Studio, LLC.
Direct inquiries to Black Lake Press at www.blacklakepress.com.

ISBN 978-0-9824446-0-3

This book is dedicated to the three generations of men who make me want to be a better man.

To my grandfather, the late Harold Langejans: His faith, wisdom, generosity and selflessness are virtues that I strive to adopt, and I pray that my generation will as well. I only wish I had appreciated this more while he was still here.

To my father, Steve Stam: I'm hard on your generation in this book. Thanks for being the exception. I have no idea how a man who grew up with no father became such a great one himself, but I thank you for figuring it out.

To my son, Isaiah Stam: You are my daily motivation to grow and influence my generation to be worthy parents to your generation. I pray that you will realize at a much earlier age than I did, the value of the wisdom that is all around you from people like the two men above.

Table of Contents

Acknowledgments

In any person's life there are many, probably hundreds, of people who deserve acknowledgement for playing a role in helping that person become who he is. My life is no exception, and it would take dozens of pages to even begin expressing my gratitude. As it relates directly to this book and my personal journey described in it, there are a couple people who I want to clearly acknowledge by name.

First and always, to my wife: thank you for sticking with me through all of this. You not only helped me write a book, but you chose to stay by my side through the real-life story told in it, even though it was one that you would probably just as soon not played a role in. I love you.

To Grandma "Golf" (the nickname my son bestowed upon her when he was three): thank you for encouraging me to make this book a reality. It would have not been written had it not been for you. Thanks for demonstrating your commitment to faith and to family. Thank you for being an example of how to live right.

To my co-author, friend and mentor Greg: thank you for being honest with me for over ten years. For befriending me even after I ignored your advice and for mentoring me when I finally realized how badly I needed it. You're a wise and talented man and I can only hope that through all your future writings and teachings, more people will realize that wisdom and talent as much as I have.

To my parents, my parents-in-law, my siblings, and extended family: Thank you for your unconditional love and acceptance, your help, and your patience as you've watched and participated in the dream that one day I might actually grow up. And specifically to my Mom, thank you for worrying about me.

Finally, a sincere thank you to handful of people who have been an active part of my life, part of my story, and part of this book. I will not embarrass you by name, but you know who you are:

To those who chose to forgive;

To those who cared enough to be honest, even though honesty can hurt;

To those who cared enough to give a pat on the back;

To those who gave your time to help me become a better person;

To all of you who said: "it will be all right" and to those who said: "you better make it right;"

To those who gave your time and your thoughts to help make this a better book, hoping that in turn it might help make people better.

I thank you all from the bottom of my heart.

Rob Stam
January 2010

A Note from the Author

Standing in front of a group of people with a microphone, or writing pages in a book is always a humbling experience. Perhaps that's because you make yourself vulnerable, or perhaps it's just hard to balance honesty with the need to be liked. In my case I'll go a step further and say that telling my story is somewhat embarrassing. I don't really want to tell you about the foolish and self-serving things I've done, as they're not exactly the things one wants to hang his hat on. But, for some reason I feel that I must.

I wrote this book because as I look around I see my story being lived out across our nation. Sometimes on a much smaller scale, sometimes on a much larger scale that even attracts media attention. But the story is essentially the same. America has been an example of progress for many years. On one hand we have come so far, on the other we have gotten so far away from what we were supposed to be.

My desire is not to portray myself as some great American success story about a guy who got back on his feet after a financial collapse to become a winner again in business. My goal is to simply offer something of value that someone, somewhere benefits from. I hope that's you. I struggled for quite some time determining what shape this book would take. Then, one day my uncle gave me some great words of wisdom. He said: "Rob, write it as if you were writing it just for your son."

Sometimes I come home after my boy is asleep. I go into his room and sit on the side of his bed. It's hard not to shed a tear as I watch him sleep. I had no idea what love was until I became a father. As a Christian, it changed everything. As a person, it gave me a new level of responsibility.

A friend of mine told me about a lesson he learned while studying Austrian economics: Every choice a human makes is based on value. So, to my son and to all of you I would say this: never stop digging deeper to discover what actually has value. Chances are you won't find it among the masses. You won't find it from the media and you probably won't even find it in school. But, it exists for those who authentically seek it. Whether you share my faith or aren't even sure where these words come from, you'll have to admit that this is good advice about seeking what is truly valuable: "Whatever is true, whatever is noble, whatever is right, whatever is pure, whatever is lovely, whatever is admirable--if anything is excellent or praiseworthy--think about such things."

Introduction
"A Long Time Ago in a Village Far, Far Away..."

I grew up with *Star Wars.*

I'm a member of "Generation X," kids born between the early 1960s and the late 1970s. Most of us were somewhere between diapers and ninth grade when the first *Star Wars* movie came out. I think it's safe to say that for the last twenty-plus years *Star Wars* has been the single biggest cultural phenomenon that we've known. The movies, toys, books, cartoons, video games, Halloween costumes, thousands of jokes and parodies—well, they've been with us always. *Star Wars* is a fixture of our landscape, like a mountain or coastline next to our town.

We grew up during the longest period of economic growth in American--heck, maybe even in world--history. When the first *Star Wars* movie came out the Dow Jones Industrial Average was around

900 points; when the last movie was released it was more than 10,000. Our parents' 401ks got fat, and the little houses that we had collected our *Star Wars* toys in became worth ten times what mom and dad had paid for them. Lots of us borrowed from good old mom and dad, who had portfolios and home equity to spare. We had none, but figured it was only a matter of time before we got ours, too.

Our generation saw the Information Age begin and the Cold War end, but those weren't our accomplishments. It all happened around us, not because of us, but we assumed that life just worked that way.

Star Wars shaped our imaginations, and we imagined that we lived in that type of a universe. Lots of us voted for Barack Obama because we naturally assume that Luke Skywalker-like optimism and Jedi smarts can change anything. We can't define the "Force," but we are sure that things will turn out OK if we've got it.

Now we're in our thirties and forties. We're hitting the age when we start running for Congress and running major corporations. As the legions of baby boomers retire to live out their eternal grooviness with megadoses of Viagra and iPod's full of classic rock, it's going to be our turn to lead America.

Are we ready?

That's what this book is about. Is the *Star Wars* generation ready for the real challenges that America faces? Do we even know what they are? Has our experience as a generation prepared us to know what to do, much less to actually do it? We tend to think of "change" as something exciting because our generation has only known changes for the better. But over the centuries there have been plenty of generations that faced changes that they couldn't understand or even see coming.

Let me give you an example of such a generation. It happened in a long time ago in a village far, far away...

It was probably fun to be a young adult in the village of Farnham during the summer of 1348.

We might find it primitive and boring, but for a young man or woman in a village in rural England, life was as good as it could get at that point in history. Farnham is in Surrey County, in southeast England, and in the mid-fourteenth century the weather was nicer than that part of the world would see for another six hundred years. It was near the end of something called the Medieval Warm Period, right before the Little Ice Age, and for hundreds of years warm weather meant longer growing seasons that produced bumper crops throughout Europe. More crops meant more food and that meant more people. Families got bigger and so did villages like Farnham. So big, in fact, that for the last couple of centuries land was always being cleared and new farming villages were popping up throughout Britain.

In 1347 England had more people and money than it had ever known before. It was the pinnacle of medieval culture: castles dotted the land, great cathedrals were going up and knighthood--with all its chivalry, falconry and jousting--was as fascinating as it would ever become.

That summer would have been particularly thrilling for any young boy who daydreamed about knights, battles and adventure. Over the winter news had reached Farnham that Edward the III, the dynamic king who had brought stability and success to England for the last twenty years, had defeated the French at Crécy in northern France. Vastly outnumbered, British long-bowmen had mown down wave after wave of mounted French knights. The flower of France's nobility, the most fearsome military force in Europe at the time, was destroyed by citizen-soldiers from villages across Britain. A thirteen-year-old boy from Farnham couldn't really aspire to becoming a knight, but greater prosperity and better diet made it possible for him to own and to master a deadly longbow. It's not hard to imagine boys hiding among the rows of growing barley that summer, firing toy bows at each other. For them, it might have been like hearing that a scrappy bunch of X-Wing fighters had taken down the Death Star. Someday, perhaps, country boys like them would take their fathers' longbows, journey to distant France, and defeat a charge of armored knights.

In the summer of 1348 the young men and women of Farnham anticipated taking their turn as the heads of households and the leaders of the village. They understood the economics of feudal tenant farming, homes crowded with large families and the social order that had been in place for hundreds of years. Young men anticipated taking their father's place on the farm or in the workshop. Girls looked forward to having and caring for lots of kids. They knew the challenges of their generation and were ready for them.

They were wrong.

A few years earlier, a bacteria called *Yersinia Pestis* had infected some fleas in China. The fleas climbed onto the backs of rats, who in turn hitchhiked along the trade routes to the Mediterranean. The globetrotting bacteria then hopscotched from the Italian merchant cities across the known world. Wherever they went they brought something that no one had expected in the boom years of the early 1300s: bubonic plague.

The Black Death reached England through the port of Weymouth in June of 1348. The bacteria-ridden fleas only had to ride grain carts and unwashed bodies a hundred miles across the green pastures of southern England to arrive in Farnham by October. That month the villagers began dying.

When the Plague hit Farnham there were perhaps a thousand tenant families. By the end of 1350, twenty-four months after it arrived, upwards of a third of them were gone. In the congested cities it killed half the population. It was common for a person to bury all the members of his family and have to figure out what to do next. Over a four-year period the Black Death killed something like 50% of the people living in Europe and the Middle East. Bam. Just like that. It would take hundreds of years for the population of Britain to recover to what it had been in the summer of 1348.

Aside from the tragic loss of life, the Black Death caused all sorts of unforeseen changes in Medieval society. In Farnham it altered the relationship between owners and tenants, management and labor, producers and consumers. All of a sudden estates and wealth were frequently changing hands. The law and social relationships had to adapt. Lots of highly skilled people disappeared and were replaced by others with less training and experience.

A society that was (relatively) rich and crowded was turned upside down almost over night. While everyone suffered human loss, some folks came out of it with more money and power: the labor shortage helped create what we would call a middle class, and many women were also empowered after they became the only ones left to inherit the family estate. The nobility even had to impose wage controls to keep the cost of labor under control. The Church was affected when experienced priests died while ministering to the sick, and their positions were quickly filled by uneducated and unmotivated recruits. Fields went unplanted and villages were abandoned. In Farnham the first wave of the Plague tapered off by the end of 1350. The village survived, but life in it was very different from what it had been just two years before.

Here's my point about Farnham: the young adults there (in those days it would have been people in their late teens or twenties) expected to become the leaders of a village with a familiar way of life. It was almost their time to become the heads of households, the chief craftsmen, the landlords, the estate managers, whatever. But when their turn came they became the leaders of a place very different from that in which they were raised. Economics, law, business, religion, culture: nothing was what they expected it to be. They had to innovate, to invent new (or rediscover old) ways of being a village together.

They adapted. They survived. Society moved forward in ways--for better or for worse--than anyone could have imagined during that last, golden summer of 1348.

In the next few years the *Star Wars* generation is going to get its chance to lead. We're going to face challenges we never imagined or wanted. Every generation is tested. Will we pass ours?

Let me clear up two possible misunderstandings right away. This book is not predicting plagues, zombie outbreaks, meteor strikes or alien invasions. Just as the young men and women of Farnham never anticipated the challenges that they would face in their lifetimes, neither can we. We should be aware of the fact that, until this point, we have lived during a remarkable season in history, and seasons change. They don't always change for the better, at least not for the people living through those changes. We need to be ready and willing to question our assumptions and adjust our lives to take on problems that we never saw coming even a few years ago.

The second possible misunderstanding is that this book only applies to Generation X. The problems we face are America's problems, not Gen X's problems. Age didn't matter in Farnham during 1348: everyone had to cope with the Plague and its effects. But it was younger adults who were in the position of leading the community through the changes that came. In the same way, while Boomers and Generation Y and everyone else will have to face the same problems, those born in the 60's and 70's will have to lead America through whatever happens over the next twenty years.

Almost Our Time

It's about time for us to face some things that we've been avoiding, because it's almost our time to be responsible for them.

Chapter 1
"Chapter Seven"

This was a tough room.

Admittedly, there weren't chains on the walls or loose car batteries to shock your privates. But by the time I got to this room I'd already been beaten into submission. This room is for after you've been defeated.

It was one of those bland government rooms in one of those bland government buildings. In a weird way that made it worse than if the place looked like Abu Ghraib. In a place like that you probably take solace in the fact that you're a victim of injustice. All this order and functional furniture just reminds you that it's your fault, that you're a failure.

I was angry that my wife had to sit here with me, but I could only be angry at myself. I may have failed, but she never did. My belly flop was so ginormous that I'd sucked her into the black hole of my failure.

I thought of that scene in the movie Jerry McGuire: *"You see this jacket I'm wearing? I don't really need it. Because I'm cloaked in failure! I'm a cautionary tale..."*

As if to make the point, our attorney had called and said that she couldn't show up, so she was sending some fill-in attorney guy in her place. And he was nowhere to be found. I'm telling you: *cloaked in failure.*

So we sat in the chairs in the back and watched other couples take their turn. It was all very clinical and seemed sort of harmless. Come up to the trustee's desk, take a seat, answer his questions. It was the fact that you had to be there in the first place that was so eviscerating and humiliating. My wife and I had nothing better to do than eavesdrop, and we heard these husbands and wives trying to explain themselves, to give their version of how they ended up sitting at this table.

I couldn't help but wonder about the trustee behind the desk. He seemed like a nice enough guy, like a grandpa in some family classic movie: tough but fair, efficient but patient. What off-ramps had he taken on life's interstate to spend his day sifting through people's screw-ups for $60 a case?

The trustee was businesslike. He'd sift through a file, ask some questions, make some decisions, and he was done. He'd get up and shuffle out. Go and sin no more.

Chapter Seven

I couldn't help thinking that our case wouldn't be so easy. Why? Because we were worse than all the others? I don't know, maybe just because nothing had gone easily for years. If anything could get screwed up it did. Usually by me, or by people that I allowed to screw things up: so, in effect, by me. Ever since we realized that we'd driven off the edge of the cliff and were going to have to declare bankruptcy, nothing had gone smoothly. By that I don't mean that we should have been able to wave a little white towel and see the mess I made go away overnight. Yet this whole process had been like an Easter-egg hunt from Hell: we'd go looking for some document we needed or try to resolve some contract and get surprised by fresh horrors that we knew nothing about. As we sat there, watching other people pay their pound of flesh and be allowed to limp on with their life, I had this sick feeling that it wouldn't go that easily when "grandpa" called us up to the desk.

Our fill-in attorney showed up half an hour late. Uncle Rico. I called him that because he reminded me of the dude from Napoleon Dynamite. Actually, he was a pretty nice guy, but he looked like he lived in a van and sold Tupperware door-to-door. When he wasn't fill-in attorneying, of course. A few years earlier I had fancy lawyers with fancy cars and fancy offices. Now all I could afford was Uncle Rico. Welcome to bankruptcy.

After an hour it was our turn to shuffle up to the Desk of Justice. Grandpa hit a button on his tape recorder and started asking questions about our income, about all the companies I had in my name over the last five years, about all the real estate I'd bought. I was supposed to explain how I'd leveraged everything against everything else, borrowed against borrowed assets, like some sort of perpetual motion machine made of credit cards and equity lines. I'm still not completely sure that I can explain it. You had to be there.

But enough of my past: "grandpa" wanted to know about today and tomorrow as well. *What did I own, right now? I'm working in sales at the moment? Really...what do I sell? How do I get paid? Does anyone owe me any money? Any commissions being held back until after the Chapter 7, hmmmm?* More darkly, *am I hiding any assets? Am I conspiring to keep income away from my creditors? And, by the way, what are my future plans?* You mean after the uncomfortable walk to the car and ride home with my wife?

He did his job and did it well, always making eye contact as if he could see through us. There was no way to not be completely transparent with this guy, even if honesty was going to hurt you.

Actually, my instinct wasn't to clam up at all, I wanted to spill my guts. I wanted to tell every backstory, confess every misdeed, explain all my screw-ups, unburden myself of every sordid detail. I wanted grandpa to listen and understand and tell me that I'm not a bad person. I never wanted this to happen, never wanted to sit here in this bland room with his tape recorder running and my fill-in attorney sitting on one side and my hurt and confused wife on the other. Had I even thought for a second that it would turn out this way, well... I would never had played with those bad kids. I wanted grandpa to know that I had foolishly trusted people and those people turned out to be crooked. My mother had warned me--had asked me if everyone was jumping off a cliff would I do it to?--and I had told her of course not. But then I went ahead and launched all those LLC's and tried to flip all those houses and bought all that stuff because everyone around me was doing it. And if they were doing it, it must be OK. Surely, grandpa would understand that.

Does waterboarding make you talk like this? Sitting in front of grandpa with Uncle Rico and my wife watching, I would have told him the formula for some secret rocket fuel if I had known it.

Grandpa really didn't care about my need for absolution. He wasn't my Grandpa anyway, that was my own weird psycho-projection thing. This guy was a Chapter 7 bankruptcy trustee and all he needed to know was what I had left and how much of it he could take in order to give all my creditors a couple cents back on the dollars I had borrowed. That might have been the most humbling part of it all. Like the Elephant Man I wanted to shout, "I am a human being!" but in the eyes of Federal Bankruptcy Court I was damaged goods, a diminished pile of assets to be sorted through to find anything left of value.

I guess that was fair. When I was signing all those loan papers, credit card receipts and mortgages I never really thought of the people whose 401ks were bundled into those loans. I wanted cash, and I signed for it. Now they wanted whatever was left of their cash back.

The weird thing is that it had all been such a tangled mess that I really didn't understand--still don't--all the details of the financial house of cards we'd built. I couldn't answer all of Grandpa's questions with a sufficient ring of confidence. File this away for future reference: if you're ever in bankruptcy court, don't look or sound uncertain. It makes you look like you're hiding something.

As complicated as our case was, it didn't take long for him to sniff out some potentially questionable areas. It was like a cop show where the detective smells something fishy, and the perp just squirms. Except that in this case, I really wasn't hiding anything. My mess was just so disorganized that I didn't really understand it well enough to explain it.

At one point the trustee implied that, depending upon how I answered a question, it could mean some type of fraud. He didn't do the wink-wink-nudge-nudge thing, but he made sure that I got the drift. Great, I thought, out of the frying pan and into the fire. Then his inner grandpa took over for a minute, and he was kind enough to adjourn the session and give us a chance to update our Chapter 7 bankruptcy petition so that it wouldn't blow up in our faces. It was very kind of him. He didn't have to do that.

We got up and shuffled out, past other couples waiting to approach the confessional. They may have watched us go, envying us that our ordeal was over, but of course it wasn't. The court needed more information, I needed to go back and unravel more clues about what I had done. There was more paperwork to file. I needed to talk to my real attorney, not my fill-in attorney. It just never stopped.

I can only imagine what my wife was feeling. This was supposed to be the day that this would all be over and, once again, nothing happened the simple way. She had nothing to do with any of these financial shenanigans; she was only there because she was my wife who had supported me without question and hadn't left me when it all started unraveling. Her reward was being dragged into this mess.

Chapter Seven

Fortunately, the parking meter hadn't expired. Getting a parking ticket while you're in bankruptcy court? Talk about an "epic fail." But the handful of change we'd dug out of the ashtray when we arrived had sustained us. There was a metaphor in there somewhere, I was sure.

That morning we had left our son with a babysitter, and as we drove the 30 minutes back to pick him up I realized that the tension between us had become the new normal. Today was just another episode. When would we get to the series finale?

Driving away from the court--not for the last time, apparently--I wondered how I had gotten here. How had I screwed up the money thing so badly? A few years back I had a pretty wife, a cute baby, a nice house, a good job. But there was a buzz in the air: everyone around me said I could have more. It seemed that everyone I knew was starting a company, and the banks couldn't hand out small business loans fast enough. Not only could I have a bigger house, I could have it built for me, customized to my tastes and idiosyncrasies. No cash? No documentation of income? No problem. Everyone knew a mortgage guy, and everyone was refinancing every six months. Real estate was an investment, smart people were flipping houses. There were actually house-flipping shows on cable to show you how. And if flipping a little was good, flipping a lot must be better. I tried to flip seven.

And so on, and so on and so on. I wondered how I ended up in Chapter Seven Federal Bankruptcy. Heck, I wondered how so many of us did, from ordinary folks like me to the biggest corporations in America.

How did we all get here? And where do we go now?

Chapter 2
"The Society of the Spectacle"

It's just human nature: people have always loved a good show. The ancient Greeks had huge amphitheaters for sophisticated dramas and comedies, with sets, costumes and actors being lowered onstage with rigging. Every four years the Greeks would gather to watch naked athletes compete in the Olympic Games (that could boost ratings today!). The Etruscans (ancestors of the Romans) came up with the tradition of gladiatorial games. The Romans, of course, took all of this and ran with it, thus the Coliseum, chariot races, and all the rest. In fact, when the urban masses in Rome got restless, some of the emperors kept them distracted with "bread and circuses," free gladiatorial spectacles with free food at the stadium. Pack 'em in, fill 'em up and keep 'em from rioting outside the palace.

Human nature hasn't changed since then. We all love a spectacle: jousts, parades, athletic competitions, religious services, world's fairs, concerts, coronations, beheadings, riots, elections, American Idol, car chases on TV and whatever Paris Hilton has done this week. At our best moments this stuff inspires us, at our worst it titillates our nastier inclinations, and most of the time it just distracts us from the boredom of daily life.

So there's nothing new about our desire for this stuff. What *is* relatively new is its availability and how it dominates our culture. We have become the Society of the Spectacle.

I wish that I had coined that term, but the honor goes to a French Marxist writer and filmmaker, of all people. Let's be clear: I'm not French and I'm not a Marxist. Guy Debord published *Society of the Spectacle* in 1967 as a Marxist critique of western capitalism. It contributed to the rationale for the 1968 riots in Paris. I don't buy into all of that, but even a broken clock is right twice a day, and Debord made some pretty valid observations, which I think we ought to pay attention to, even if we don't accept the conclusions he draws from them.

Guy Debord was way ahead of his time, almost prophetic, on one important point. The irony is that in order to understand it we have to refer to the Baby Boom generation's greatest fear.

When President Dwight Eisenhower retired he famously warned that we needed to be on the lookout, lest the "Military-Industrial Complex" control the direction of our society. This was the sometimes conspiratorial but always self-serving partnership between the government and corporations that would make enemies and fight wars to profit from tax dollars. They would (and maybe have) manipulate our culture and politics for their own profit. That became the rallying cry for the Baby Boom generation, and lots of them have been on the lookout for it ever since. It has come to dominate our popular culture: how many times have you seen the villain in a movie, TV show, novel, comic book or whatever turn out to be the sinister, shadowy "military-industrial complex?" Seriously, it's just about the only real boogeyman we have in our culture.

In *Society of the Spectacle* this obscure, French Marxist argued that there was another powerful conglomeration manipulating us for its own profit: the Media-and-Advertising Complex. In 1967 he saw how television was coming to dominate modern life, so that we begin to experience life through the television screen rather than directly living it. We have, Debord said, become a society of spectacle: dominated by whatever is presented to us through media and advertising.

In the forty-something years since Debord made that observation, hasn't it become even more true? He could never have foreseen the technology that has sped up the process of filling every aspect of our lives with media images. I was born nine years after he wrote his book, and my generation has known nothing but a media spectacle. While baby-boomer parents were out either working for or against the Military-Industrial Complex, we were raised by the Media-Advertising Complex. Network television became 24-hour cable, pinball machines became video games and so on. The Internet? Do I even need to say it?

Debord said that in the society of the spectacle people don't have actual life experiences, they live through media presentations of life. Now I sound like an old codger, but even when I was a kid we played ping-pong or lawn darts or went to a bowling alley. There was at least an actual experience involved: you put on the ugly rented shoes and had to find a ball with finger holes that fit. Today we don't bother; we play video versions of all those games. There are even video games of board games: you can play Monopoly or checkers on a screen. How is that easier?

I've been a musician since I was a kid. I love to play piano and guitar, and write music. Is there anything that makes Debord's point more clearly than *Guitar Hero?* As a society we don't even bother to learn to play an instrument anymore: we play through an avatar who plays a video game of playing an instrument. Even if you want to record a real song in a real studio, we can use digital technology to tune your off-pitch voice. In our world, you don't even need to be able to sing to record.

A lot of us born near the end of Generation X first paid attention to war when we watched the whole thing broadcast on TV, like a reality series, during Gulf War I in 1991. Some of us first began to pay attention to politics when we heard people on TV talking about the president receiving oral sex in the Oval Office. We learn about history from movies and about sex from online porn. We find our mates through E-Harmony. We don't know our neighbors because our real neighborhood, truth be told, is our virtual one on Facebook.

We see and experience life through video rectangles: TV's, computers, cell phones.

So what? Didn't I start by saying that people have always been drawn to spectacles? Was it really better to learn about the world through books and newspapers? Was it really better to watch a joust or a parade than American Idol? Was it really better to play a board game than play a video game? Was it really better to write letters and mail them than to just Facebook or video chat?

I don't know if it was better or worse, but we should really think about some of the implications of living this way.

First, technology has compressed time and space in our lives. Imagine some sort of spectacle from a previous age: a high mass at a cathedral, or a county fair, or a public hanging. Exciting stuff, no doubt. But the laws of physics kept those spectacles within check in our lives. The event was some distance away, it only took place so often, and it took time to go there. Entertainment and distraction could only consume so much of us. Throughout most of human history the average person spent most of his or her life engaged in physically doing things: eating, writing, working, walking, talking, whatever. Maybe every Sunday you walked an hour to the cathedral, saw the great mass, and it made an impression on you; then you walked the hour home where you ate with your family and milked a cow or something. There was a natural limit to how much we could be entertained and distracted.

Now? On your laptop you can see and do things that in previous generations a kid had to join the navy and go to some distant port to experience. Technology has allowed the Media-Advertising Complex 24/7 access to every aspect of our lives. There is nowhere that they are not. We are naked before them.

What percentage of your life--your waking hours, your activities, and your "mindshare"--are exposed to the Spectacle of media, marketing and advertising? What about your children? Maybe a better question is, "Is there anyplace in your life that isn't exposed? A refuge from the noise and glare of it all?" Maybe when we go for a walk. Except most of us don't walk, and when we do, how many of us are jacked into our iPods? At church? Again, most of us don't bother to go anyway. When we do, lots of us are at a contemporary church with video screens and rock music, designed to make us feel "comfortable" by keeping us immersed in electronic media. The shower just may be the last refuge for most of us, the only time during our day when we aren't naked before the electromagnetic waves from some speaker or screen.

That's the second thing to think about: the media and advertising industries are not looking out for our welfare. They're not necessarily evil, but they are for-profit. They produce all these images for their benefit, not ours. Again, there's nothing necessarily wrong with that. If I make widgets and I hire marketers and advertisers to help me sell my widgets, I expect them to do their best. We are constantly being persuaded to believe in things so that we'll buy things.

I'm not saying that there isn't a Military-Industrial Complex. I'm sure that we've spent tax dollars on some weapons we didn't need to buy and spilled blood in wars we didn't need to fight. We are right to be wary. But while the baby boomers, our parents' generation, obsessed about that, they helped build the Media-Advertising Complex. From the Beatles' first appearance on Ed Sullivan, through Woodstock, the video porn industry, the Superbowl commercials, designer t-shirts, Disneyland, Blockbuster Video and the megachurches, the Boomers couldn't get enough Spectacle. It fed the narcissism of their generation: *all this entertainment was for them!* Like the spoiled rich girl in *Willy Wonka* who wants daddy to buy her an Oompa Loompa, they thought it was all about feeding their constant need for entertainment. And they plopped us down in front of TV's while they went out and got more stuff.

We learned the lesson. We became consumers, and the most significant influence in our lives has been pop-culture media. It's our only real culture, our only reference point, our mother tongue. Without pop-culture media, we are nothing.

I repeat: all of this is not created for our benefit. It is created to sell us things. Previous generations may have gone to a play or a horse race or a carnival. We have been *raised in* a carnival. We've never been outside the carnival, in which everything is a pitch and everything is for sale. Don't say it hasn't affected us.

Our generation came up with a new disease: Attention Deficit Hyperactivity Disorder, or ADHD. Sometimes the images, the spectacle, doesn't cycle fast enough for us. Some of us have a hard time focusing on any one thing for very long. We need to change the channel.

My story has been wrapped up with the Spectacle. It's how I ended up bankrupt, in more ways than one.

After high school I tried college, mostly to please my parents. I didn't fit in and I didn't belong, probably because I craved the Spectacle. I think that I might have had ADHD. I got bored easily and

I didn't like to read books. I was convinced that there was nothing that I couldn't learn "out there," from the Society of the Spectacle.

So I dropped out and became a salesman, for something I understood: the media spectacle. I started working with a company that designed and installed the latest and greatest audio and video systems, mostly in churches. In the 1990s churches were starting to notice that not too many Gen Xers were coming to church. They weren't stupid: they saw the difference between our generation's mass-media culture and the no-media culture of the Church. A lot of churches, in an earnest desire to reach out to Gen X, thought that they needed to bring mass-media culture into worship. Gen X likes TV? Cool, put giant TV screens at the front of church and run them continually through the service. Replace pews with movie theater seats. Put in rock concert audio systems, and show close ups of the electric guitar player on the big screen during his solo. Hire producers to put the church announcements into video "packages" that could run between the songs, just like TV commercials. Sell designer T-shirts, hats and DVDs at the concession stand in the lobby. Bring Gen X's world into the church and Gen X will feel comfortable in the church. If we build it, they will come.

I became a star in this world. I not only knew the technology and had the sales skills, I believed in it. Shortly after dropping out of college, I was 21-22 years old and making over $100k a year selling churches these kinds of systems. I was traveling all over the country, flying first class, going to trade shows, eating in awesome restaurants, going to Las Vegas to see concerts. In fact, we were going to Vegas to figure out how to bring that type of spectacle into churches: what brand of speakers systems, what kind of video projectors were they using in the Vegas theaters? How can we bring that level of "excellence" into churches?

It validated my choice to drop out of college. Why sit in dull lectures, reading hundreds of pages from college professors who made $50k when I could change the Church from the inside out, reach my generation and get rich while doing it? Why be bored in college when I could run around with the crowd that put on rock tours, produced records, and made TV shows? Honest truth: I loved the spectacle like a crackhead loves his pipe, and I believed in the Society of the Spectacle.

Eventually I ended up owning the company. I went in with a partner and we acquired it from the previous owner. While we were at it we started our own music-recording studio and record label. We bought expensive cars, we built custom houses, and we wore designer clothes. We were invested in the Spectacle, baby, and we figured that there was nowhere to go but up.

Here's the thing about the Society of the Spectacle: it isn't real. None of it. It's the appearance of life, not life itself. We think that we're relevant or successful or important or loved if we imitate what we see through our rectangular screens. But we may have no authentic experiences of our own and no genuine relationships with other human beings. Certainly, if we are exposed to it long enough, we may have no original thoughts. Our identity is an imitation of what we see and hear. We don't know what we like or what we believe or what we love apart from what we are being sold.

The warning signs were there, but they conflicted with the spectacle I was caught up in. We borrowed way, way too much money to fund the company. I saw images of moguls and entrepreneurs and tried to imitate them without really understanding business principles like they did. Like an actor who copies the accent and mannerisms of some famous person to portray him, I wasn't a mogul, I just played one like on TV. I was a poseur. But that was enough in the days when the banks couldn't lend money fast enough. Drive up in a Lexus, drop your designer sunglasses in the breast pocket of your designer suit, slouch in the bankers office like the guys on TV do, sign the loan documents like this was a movie. I was living a role I had seen on TV and so were the bankers. The Society of the Spectacle.

I even got into flipping houses, in a town where real estate values don't rise like they do on the coasts, so there was no real possibility of "flipping." But at that time there were TV series' about house flipping. I was living what I watched on TV. I borrowed and bought several of them. Again, the banks bought into the spectacle, everyone was doing it on TV, so...float the loan.

I spoke at business meetings as a model entrepreneur: I had five companies. You know how you could tell they were real? They had websites. The Society of the Spectacle.

In the end it was, is, unsustainable. Somehow, someway, we have to unplug the electronics and walk away. Love and be loved by people apart from media images. Decide what we want to own apart from branding. Listen to other people speak, read what other people write, even if that takes time. Hear ourselves think. Figure out what we really believe.

Chapter 3
"Affluenza"

I know a couple that spent fifty-something thousand dollars on credit cards and has nothing to show for it. I mean nothing. No cool furniture or designer clothes. No home theater or vacation photos from Paris. They just dribbled it away at Target and Costco, eating out, putting gas in the car, renting movies at Blockbuster. In fact, I've known a lot of people like this. The total debt load might be ten grand or sixty (or more), but none of them really have anything to show for it.

We used to think of debt like this as the price tag for big things we couldn't really afford: fancy cars, a vacation home, a boat, trips to the Caribbean. We'd draw some moral conclusion to the story about champagne tastes and beer budgets. Some of us would take a sort of perverse pleasure at the thought of someone's Ferrari being repossessed or their Rolex ending up at a pawnshop. Those were the just deserts for social climbers aspiring to live beyond their class.

But something changed as Gen X grew up. Actually, several factors came together to create a society where ordinary people can pile up a lifetime's worth of debt at big box stores, chain restaurants and gas stations. It's not what you might think, either. It's not because our society is too expensive and people are too poor to live in it.

In fact, it's exactly the opposite: never before in human history have consumer goods been cheaper and people been richer, than right now. We live in a golden age of human economic history. Even in the midst of the recession at the time this book is being written, no generation since humans started walking upright has had more or better food, clothing, housing, transportation, entertainment, hard goods or health care than we do. And certainly no generation has ever had the buying power that we do.

So how can all this stuff be so cheap (relatively) and so many of us be so broke?

For starters, consider the marketplace around us, the greatest that the world has ever known. We can get virtually anything from anywhere at a staggeringly low price point. Manufacturing technologies, globalization, shipping infrastructure and economies of scale make consumer goods almost comically abundant. Everything from clothing to cookware to cellphones is cheap and plentiful. Until recently the kings of Europe couldn't have sat on a sofa as comfortable as ours, watching entertainment as dazzling as what we see everyday on our television, and ordered through a magic box (our laptops opened to Amazon or eBay) whatever they fancied as easily as we do, only to have it arrive on their doorstep the next day. And the kings of Europe can only do it now by using the same tools we do (although they probably have someone click the mouse for them).

Gen Xers can hardly imagine that before we were born, getting stuff wasn't all that easy. Through most of human history there were speed bumps on the road to buying things: cost, time, distance, etc. If you wanted something you had to, to some degree or another, save for it, go somewhere to get it or wait for it to come to you. Those speed bumps slowed consumer traffic. More to our point, they probably also slowed down purchasing decisions. It took a little more effort to blow your money.

The Industrial Revolution began to mass produce some consumer goods in the early 1800s, but not everything was mass produced on the sheer scale that it is today. Not only that, but there weren't the means to connect consumers to manufacturers that we now take for granted.

In the 1880s farmers scattered across the USA bought manufactured goods from general stores in the fall when they came to town to sell their crops. Each little store in each little town could only afford to buy and inventory a few things, so the choices were limited and the prices unpredictable. In 1888 Richard Sears published the first Sears Catalogue, allowing farmers to sit at home and browse through hundreds of pages of clothes, sewing machines, tools, home furnishings and just about anything else they could imagine. There were pictures and descriptions, and the prices were clearly stated.

Families across the nation could total up an order, save up the money and mail it to the central Sears office in Chicago with payment. A few weeks later it would arrive. We can hardly believe what a really big deal the Sears catalogue was, or what the first department store chains like Montgomery Wards represented.

Even so, marketing goods through advertising and printed catalogues sent through the mail was expensive. One of the reasons why the U.S. Postal Service is in deep financial difficulty is that its revenue model relied heavily on all those catalogues and advertisements. Junk mail was the Post Office's bread and butter until just a few years ago.

Traditionally, the costs to warehouse and ship products added a lot to the price. During Gen X's lifetime, communications have allowed manufacturers to quickly adjust their inventories, and our transportation networks allow us to have fresh produce year-round because the apples and oranges can be flown in from South America.

The Consumer Revolution isn't just for new, mass-produced goods, either. The infrastructure of modern commerce allows us to find the most trivial replacement parts or collect the most obscure used junk through eBay.

File this as the first reason that so many of us are in so much debt: *Gen Xers are the first humans to grow up able to buy just about anything, from anywhere, anytime...for next to nothing.*

The second thing that has gotten so many of us into this mess was easy credit. There have always been people willing to take the deed to your family farm in return for a loan. Shakespeare's *The Merchant of Venice* is about a guy who wants to borrow money to buy a shipload of merchandise overseas, bring it to Italy and sell it for a profit. The banker, Shylock, makes the loan, but he hates the merchant Antonio because he's secretly in love with his girlfriend. So he tells the merchant that he must secure the loan with a pound of his own flesh: that is, if he can't repay by the due date, Shylock will get to cut off one pound of Antonio's body (Shylock's choice as to which pound). In the story the ship sinks, the merchandise (and thus the money) is lost and...well, you should read it for yourself. The point is that it's always been possible to get that kind of loan. Small town banks used to be the place where small businessmen, farmers and homeowners went to get loans, secured by "collateral" (I use quotation marks because most Gen Xers have never had to deal with the concept).

Some Gen Xers can vaguely remember "layaway" plans from our childhood. We would want a new bike or a winter coat from the department store. Mom would make us try it on, then take it back to the "Layaway Desk." They'd put our bike or coat in the back room with a little tag on it and Mom would give them 10% or so. She'd come in and make payments. When it was paid off, the store would take the tag off and hand us the item.

Pounds of flesh and layaway plans went away sometime in our childhoods. We could have pretty much anything we wanted whenever we wanted it through "charge" cards. They started with big chain retailers: you'd get a Sears card or a charge card for a chain of gas stations. They didn't have to work too hard to sell us all on the idea. Who wants to mess with layaway? You can have the bike or coat now. The department store will just add a monthly service charge to cover the convenience. As far as putting gas in the car, the company understands if you're a little short today. No reason to dig change out of the sofa. You could just use your gas station charge card and fill 'er up. Of course they added a little monthly service charge to cover the convenience, but you'll be on your way down the road!

Somewhere along the way it occurred to the banks that they were missing out on all these point of purchase loans. So instead of a particular store chain giving you a charge account we got credit cards, with names that conveyed how they opened doors to buy anything anywhere: *Visa! MasterCard! American Express! Discover!* No more driving around until you found a gas station that you had a charge card for, you could put it on your universal credit card.

Gen Xers were the first generation to be offered credit cards when we turned 18 years old. We got the offers in the mail right after high school graduation: good news, we had been "pre-approved." Some of us were offered them at college, from tables in the student center that gave us a T-shirt if we signed up, or in the bookstore if we bought our first semester's textbooks with a shiny new Visa card. Of course the store brands fought back: most chain retailers now require their clerks to point out that you'll save 10% on today's purchase if you'll open an account with the store.

File this as the second reason that so many of us are in so much debt: *buying stuff is so easy with instant, thoughtless credit.* We don't have to save or layaway or put up collateral. We can have anything we want, when we want it, with nothing down.

The third thing that got so many of us into this mess was our own spoiled sense of entitlement. Yeah, you read that right. And yes, I am talking to *you.*

We all understand the idea of spoiled entitlement, we're just sure it doesn't apply to us. We think of some rich kid, whose parents are celebrities or politicians or CEO's or orthopedic surgeons. We imagine the type of kids that grew up with country club memberships and got sports cars when they turned 16. The teenagers who were raised with expensive tastes and will never have to work a day in their lives. The ones who wreck the Mercedes and puke in the flower beds at the country club all over their Jimmy Choos. Brats like that are disgusting. That is so clearly not us.

OK, maybe we didn't grow up like Paris Hilton, but Gen X definitely grew up spoiled and with a sense of entitlement. Our parents, the baby boomers, helped create the Consumer Revolution we've been describing, with the world as our mall and credit cards in our pockets. We took all this consumption for granted. It was normal. We grew up during thirty years of almost continual economic growth without wars or national tragedies that affected our generation as a whole. We believed that a certain level of consumption was normal. Eating out was something that earlier generations did occasionally, but we were raised on fast food chains. We grew up in the malls that sprang up in every town, full of multiplex movie theaters offering eight or sixteen or twenty screens. We shopped for clothes with our parents' charge cards and our brand new credit cards. Ours was the first generation to not share bedrooms with siblings and to have homes with two or even three car garages.

Not all of us were raised rich, but most us grew up expecting to eat at restaurants as much or more than our parents did. We expected to be able to live in houses at least as nice as the ones that we were raised in, even if it took our parents half a lifetime to be able to afford that house. We grew up without any of the boundaries that slowed down purchase decisions for previous generations. Not only did we believe that this was normal, we felt entitled to live that normal life because we grew up in a culture that taught us that everyone should get an award and every kid should get a ribbon just for playing.

File this as the third reason that so many of us are in so much debt: *we were raised to consume, to believe that a lifestyle of consumption was normal.* We even coined terms like "retail therapy" and "shopaholic" to acknowledge that we find buying stuff to be a calming drug. It calms us down from the stresses of life, which quickly become paying for our drug.

So here's our toxic stew: we felt entitled to a consumer lifestyle. Anything we wanted was just a mouse click away and we could buy now and pay later, spend before we earned. With all this opportunity we might have chosen to be wise and disciplined, but we gorged ourselves like a fat guy at a buffet.

The tragedy is that with all this debt, most of us never got that boat or dream house or trip to Europe. We just kept loading up credit cards and transferring the balances to new cards to pay for...what? Moderately priced clothes from malls? Home furnishings, cell phones and video games? Meals at chain restaurants and movie theater popcorn? Gas and CD's? Most of us didn't try to be social climbers, middle-class folks pretending to be rich. We just indulged our middle class tastes until we were bloated and broke.

Like a farmer borrowing against next year's crops, most of us assumed that our income would grow faster than the debt. Our careers would take off and the next commission check or bonus or promotion would cover this month's charges on the Visa. Needless to say, that didn't always happen. The result is that we feel a sort of continual low-grade anxiety, a subliminal stress. It's always there, like traffic noise: the pressure to make enough money to keep up with our consumer lifestyle. We need to feed the beast, and the beast is always hungry, always growling. We misplace the blame: we talk about the pressures of modern life, we complain about the high cost of living or we whine about wages not keeping up with inflation.

The truth is that we don't really need most of this crap.

We are addicted to buying, to consuming, to borrowing. I know it's supposed to be a joke, but it's really not funny: there's a bumper sticker that reads, "I owe, I owe, so off to work I go!" We are trapped in a loop, like Bill Murray in *Groundhog Day,* never moving past the cycle of buying, consuming, borrowing and then working under stress to pay for it all.

It makes us sick. We are spiritually diseased, emotionally rattled, mentally stressed, even physically unhealthy. We buy too much, eat too much, drive too much, entertain ourselves too much and have to work too much to keep up with it.

Sociologists have come up with a term for our disease: *affluenza*. It's like the flu, but caused by our affluence. It is a lifestyle of consumerism and debt which causes us stress and disease. Affluenza is a viral contagion, spread through the Advertising Media Complex and from person to person.

I caught affluenza early, like most of my generation. Even in the conservative, midwestern town I grew up in, it was growing and spreading and infecting every aspect of our lives. Even our church, a congregation descended from stern and frugal Dutch immigrants, kept ratcheting up the spending as the economy grew and the baby-boom generation took over.

Let me give you an example: I love boats, always have and always will. In our town on the lake, I grew up around them; especially since two of the premier brands of American powerboats, Chris Craft and Tiara, were headquartered and manufactured there. My grandparents were conservative in every sense of the word, but even they traded up for a new ski boat occasionally; and I got to ride in and drive those boats from the time I was a kid. It was a no-brainer that I would own a boat of my own someday, hopefully a series of ever better boats.

When I dropped out of college and started selling sound and video systems to contemporary churches, I started making serious money for a 22 year old with no degree. More than that, I started meeting people only a couple of years older than me who had great boats. They were bigger and fancier than my grandpa's. These people had been able to buy those great boats while they were still young.

Grandpa, as much as I loved him, had worked for many years before he started buying the fancy boats.

I didn't want to work for thirty years when I could have it now and enjoy the benefits of being a young man with a fast boat. So I bought one, on credit. No big deal I thought, at the rate my career was going I'd be able to pay it off early or trade it up for a bigger and better one. And I did, getting a nicer boat with a bigger slip at the marina to go with it.

After I lost the boats on my ugly slide toward bankruptcy I had the opportunity to think about the difference between Grandpa's boats and mine. Having grown up with access to his toys I assumed that I deserved my own. But Grandpa's were the fruit of hard work, paid for with cash, a small fraction saved from a lifetime of profit. Most of his profits secured his family and helped others. My boats were unearned and grasping symbols of my spoiled sense of entitlement. His were gifts to his children and grandchildren, because it was his delight to see his family on the lake, waterskiing and making memories. Those ski boats were the just deserts of a lifetime of worthwhile work and service, building homes for the growing population of his hometown.

My boats were the symptoms of my Affluenza, and in the end they caused me nothing but stress and heartache. I still love boats, and hope to have one again someday. I hope that if and when I ever have another one it is like my grandpa's boat, a measure of my health.

None of us can be healthy if we're infected with affluenza, but none of us can heal ourselves until we recognize and accept the diagnosis. We live in the most affluent society in history with options that no humans before us have enjoyed. The problem is not our society, it's us. We lack wisdom, self-discipline and faith that life can be good without all the crap that weighs us down, but we won't let go of. It's time to get well.

Chapter 4
"Values versus Value"

To explain how I, much less America, ended up in bankruptcy court I need to talk about values. Which values, you ask? Stick with me for a couple of pages and let me explain.

I grew up neck-deep in values. Family values, Christian values, traditional American values, the value of work, *yada, yada, yada.*

My dad was the pastor of a respected church, part of a respected denomination, next to a respected Christian college in the middle of a respectable town in the Midwest. It was all very respectable. We valued respect, and respected our values.

Our town had been founded on the premise of respecting the values of Christianity, family, hard work, thrift, and ethical business. We lived in a large parsonage next door to the church, and down the block was the original city park, surrounded by restored nineteenth-century buildings. In that park is a statue of our city's founder, the Reverend Albertus Van Raalte. In the 1830s he and his followers in the Netherlands grew alarmed over the shocking lack, in their homeland, of all those values that they valued so much. Apparently, even back then Amsterdam was on its way to becoming...well, Amsterdam (if you know what I mean).

So they decided to do the whole flee-to-the-new-world/join-a-community-of-like-minded-folks thing. Like so many before and after them, they crossed the Atlantic in crummy conditions and wound up in New York, where they planned to hook up with Dutch Calvinists who had come almost two hundred years earlier. Except that when they arrived they were dismayed to discover that those earlier-arriving Dutch Calvinists had begun to abandon the values they held so dear. They had become Americanized.

Van Raalte and his followers realized that if their values weren't going to be respected then they might as well have stayed in the Netherlands. So they trudged their way into the deep woods of western Michigan, until they found a sandy, swampy stretch of Lake Michigan coastline that reminded them of their home country along the North Sea. They cleared trees and dredged swamps and built a town where their values would be respected and preserved: my town.

This story isn't unique. For three hundred years immigrants have been coming to America and forming little communities based on their particular set of values. From Plymouth Rock to Holland, Michigan to the Amana Colonies in Iowa to Little Saigon, folks who didn't like what was happening in the Old Country came to the wide, open spaces of the New World where they could cluster up with other people who shared their values. Whether it was Sicilians in Manhattan, Norwegians in Minnesota or Cubans in Miami, Americans have always formed communities based more on shared values than shared real estate. These values-based communities have been extended through all sorts of social networks: churches, unions, political parties, publications, etc.

The result is that America talks about values more than any other country. In other countries people divide along geography, race or class. Americans distrust people who don't share their values, and backslap anyone who does. Try explaining our idea of "values" to an average citizen of Paris or Shanghai or Bogota and they just don't get it. If you order a second café au lait and keep trying, you'll see a light bulb finally go off, when they realize that by "values" you mean "culture." They get it that different people have different cultures.

Now we're getting to the meat of the problem: Americans tend to use the language of "values" to describe their cultural preferences. Americans who visit France can't understand why the waiter in the café doesn't pay attention to them. The American indignantly tells his French friend that, "...hard work and customer service are American values, unlike you lazy frogs!" His French pal points out that French people prefer to be left alone in a sidewalk café, so they can read, talk or watch the pretty girls walk by.

Let me bring this home: I grew up in a town where the cultural norm was working hard at a stable job, doing business with a handshake, pinching pennies and living below one's means. These were our values. We went to church, kept our lawns mowed like fairways and bought new, mid-priced cars every two years (new to demonstrate our respectability, mid-priced to demonstrate our humility).

I was bored to death by it.

All immigrant communities in America (and maybe elsewhere) face the problem of their kids thinking that the old folks with their Old-World values are lame. Some immigrant cultures seem to be more successful than others at handing down their values through the generations, but I suspect it's a challenge for all of them.

The problem is that the kids look around and realize that they're part of a subculture, and that too many of the "values" their parents are always nagging them about are really just subcultural preferences. They realize that they have choices: they could adapt and become part of the dominant, mainstream culture, or even join another subculture. There's a whole menu of cultural options: different ways to make and spend money, to do business, to mate and marry.

Every generation thinks that its parents are lame (at least until their own kids become teenagers, then they can't comprehend why they aren't considered "cool" parents). When "values" get linked with their parents' culture then the values are considered lame as well.

That's what happened to me. I met other people who weren't from my little immigrant world. They were way cooler than the people I grew up with. They had cooler clothes and cooler cars. They dropped names of all the cool people they knew in California or New York or wherever. They talked about cooler ways to make money than by following the "values" I was raised with. They had different, cooler values. My world looked lame by comparison.

When I tried the things that they suggested, they worked. Borrow money, start companies, leverage those to buy a house, leverage that to buy six more. It was during a time when the banks couldn't hand out money fast enough. The banks were doing all sorts of cool, clever stuff like bundling debts and trading derivatives. The money kept rolling over, getting bigger like a snowball. Everyone was getting rich.

Some people tried to warn me, but the problem was that they framed the issue in terms of values. I heard things like: "These aren't the values you were raised with," or, "these aren't our values," or, "these aren't traditional American values," etc.

To which I thought, "Well, I'm bored with your values. Your values got you mid-sized homes and mid-priced cars, but there are other values out there, and those pay out faster, better and easier."

So I just opted out of the values I was raised with as if I was choosing to never eat mom's meatloaf again.

Values (plural) are subjective. They really amount to us stating our own priorities. Instead of everyone in America arguing about values, which becomes an endless shout-fest, we need to start talking about value (singular).

Value is not subjective, by definition it has actual worth. It's not what you or I prefer, it's what has a measurable quality of exchange to all of us. It's what, in the end, people actually want and need.

The concept of value applies to all spheres of our life, and when we use it as our operating principle we can live and work and do business with people who have very different cultural preferences.

This is one of the main points of this book: we need to orient our lives around creating and preserving value. That's how we will survive and thrive the economic and cultural changes that our generation faces. As long as we preserve and add value in America it will continue to be valuable. In upcoming chapters I'm going to show how this applies to education, politics, health, religion and a host of other issues.

Let's start by explaining what I mean by value in economic terms.

Traditionally, the most basic unit of economic value has been an ounce of gold. It's ironic, because gold, in and of itself, doesn't have much intrinsic value. It does have some industrial uses, to be sure, but you can't eat it, heat your house with it, it can't babysit your kids while you're at work.

No, the most basic unit of economic value in the early twenty-first century is a barrel of oil. It has actual value: it can heat a house or fuel a vehicle, it can be turned into electricity or plastic. It can be shipped, stored, or left in the ground until you decide that the time is right to take it out. If you have a barrel of oil you can trade its value for other things people want and need and will pay for.

Also, there are ways that you can add value to that barrel of oil. A barrel of oil sitting in the ground halfway around the world has value, but not as much as a gallon of gasoline in your tank or kilowatt of electricity lighting your house or a plastic fork to eat with. The person who extracts the oil adds value, the person who transports it adds value and the person who transforms it into gas or electricity or plastic adds value.

Contrast this with all the things that don't add value to the barrel of oil. The commodities trader who gambles on what price it will be tomorrow may make money, but he hasn't created or added any value to it. He may have generated wealth, but only in the sense that money changed hands and someone's portfolio got bigger. In a commodity market, for one commodity to win another one had to lose. Money changed hands, but the total wealth in the economic system didn't.

A couple of years ago the financial markets bid the price of a barrel of oil up close to $200. People placed bets based on that movement, and some people didn't realize that their retirement fund was being gambled, like an NFL betting pool, on oil prices. The value of oil, what it was really worth, hadn't changed. No one had added an extra hundred bucks of value to it by doing something creative with it.

This is what happens in a bubble economy: lots of money gets moved around, speculated on, leveraged, counted as theoretically existing. But the amount of money in the system exceeds the underlying value in the economy. My Dutch ancestors got caught up in the most famous bubble market of history: Tulip Mania, the speculation over tulip bulbs in the 1630s. Fortunes were won and lost (for a little while) as people gambled on the price of tulip bulbs, of all things (go ahead and Wikipedia it, it's quite a story). In the end, the Tulip bubble had to pop because there was no real underlying value to support all the money that had been leveraged over what were simply decorative flower seeds.

As I write this, we're living through the worst recession since the 1930s, because of another bubble market in which housing prices were speculated upward, far beyond the basic value of the actual houses. Obviously, a house has value, and there are all sorts of things that you can do to add value to a house. In fact, an entire industry, almost an entire culture, developed over housing prices, speculating, leveraging and gambling until a significant chunk of America's wealth was calculated by housing values. Last year it popped, like all bubbles do, because the pyramid had become upside down: that little three bedroom house in Los Angeles had multiple layers of bets, amounting to millions of dollars, riding on it. It couldn't support it in the end.

Like the villagers of Farnham in 1348, we never saw the disaster coming that would change our world. Here it is: America originally got rich because it was based on creating value. From growing corn to skinning beavers for their pelts, from inventing wonder drugs to creating operating systems, we got rich because we made and preserved things of actual worth.

Over the last twenty or thirty years, more and more of our economy became based on borrowing, spending, leveraging and speculating over a relatively small amount of value at the bottom of the upside-down pyramid. It wasn't, and isn't, going to be enough value to support everything we've stacked on top of it.

I have a friend whose dad grew up around cattle ranches out west. When they'd ride in a car and smell some giant field of cow manure, the kids in the back of the station wagon would always rush to roll up their windows. His dad would always take a deep whiff and say, "Hmmm. Smells like money." Now, whether cattle is profitable today is another matter, but the point is that his dad came from a time when people measured wealth in the tangible things they owned, which had intrinsic worth.

My downfall began by hanging around with people who had all the trappings of wealth: cars, clothes, houses, etc., but didn't actually produce anything of value. They were people who just moved other people's money around and speculated on other people's value. Keeping with the cow theme of the last paragraph, they were what Texans call, "All hat, no cattle."

Now it has caught up with us. Our personal debts have compiled into massive national debts. More and more of America's wealth is wrapped up in borrowing and loaning money to each other. It's a perpetual motion machine, and those never work. At the base, there has to be some energy source. Somewhere, we have to generate wealth by creating value.

I'm shocked by the number of business plans I see that are based on getting government grants. Too many people start companies without asking if they can make something that has enough value that people will actually pay for it. Instead, they calculate the worth of their product or service based on whether the government will subsidize it.

Frankly, if the government has to subsidize it with money borrowed from indebted taxpayers (or from China), it's a sure sign that the product has no real value.

So here's my modest proposal for how Generation X can begin to lead America to a better future. Let's agree to do two things.

First, let's acknowledge that there are some things which have intrinsic value, and some things that have value only to some of us. What we're going to have to do as a generation is orient our economic and political decisions around value (singular: exchangeable goods), and concede that as a pluralistic society we won't ever agree on all our values (plural: our subjective preferences).

Second, we need base our economy on creating and adding and preserving that kind of value. We need to make, invent, mine, harvest and build things that have actual worth. Our economy has to flip the pyramid right-side up so that our debt is smaller than the underlying assets that it is borrowed against.

We'll talk more about how to do those things in the next few chapters.

Chapter 5
"Vaporware"

Hero to zero in 268 days. That's got to be close to some kind of a record for a business falling to earth, making a epic crater.

It all started out so cutely. During the summer and fall of 1999 Americans started seeing commercials for a company called Pets.com. They were hosted by a goofy sock-puppet dog with a guy's arm sticking out of the bottom. The commercials were funny, and the sock puppet was *everywhere.* It showed up on all sorts of talk shows and there was even a Pets.com character balloon in the 1999 Macy's Thanksgiving Day Parade. The company ran a sock-puppet Superbowl ad in January 2000, explaining that people should buy pet supplies online from the company, "Because pets can't drive." The ad, which cost the company $1.2 million, was a hit: USA Today readers ranked it the #1 Superbowl commercial that year.

A few weeks later Pets.com made it's IPO. During the late 1990s the model for technology and "dot com" web-based companies was to launch with borrowed money, get momentum, and then "go public" by listing themselves on the NASDAQ stock exchange. The day before the stock began trading, people could buy shares in an IPO, or initial public offering. The founders, employees and venture capitalists who had funded the company's launch would get a huge payday. Pets.com's IPO, on February 10, 2000, sold 7.5 million shares at $11 per share, for a total of $82.5 million.

This was for a company that had, during the previous year, brought in $619,000 in revenue but spent $11.5 million on advertising (all that sock-puppetry wasn't cheap). They had 300 employees and had invested heavily in warehousing and infrastructure. Their business plan called for them to sell products at prices below their product and shipping costs until they could build volume and earn enough customer loyalty to be able to raise their prices to a profitable level. But they were losing an average of 20-30% per transaction. The commercials actually hurt them, as higher volume just increased their burn rate. Losing something on each sale and hoping to make it up in volume is a stupid business model that never seems to go out of style.

Even their most optimistic models didn't forecast a profit for four or five years. Until then, they counted on investors and stockholders being excited enough about the idea to keep throwing money at it. But the Dot Com bubble was popping in 2000, and the easy venture capital cash was drying up.

By fall the board realized that the ship was going down and desperately tried to sell the company, hoping that some buyer would snap it up based on the magic of the brand. There were no takers, and on the morning of November 6, 2000, the stock that had opened at $11 a share in February was trading at $0.19 a share. That afternoon, Pets.com closed its doors and announced its liquidation. Hero to zero in 268 days.

The brand was hip and they had all the right buzz with all the right people, but that wasn't enough to overcome what was basically a dumb idea: they were trying to sell fifty pound bags of dog food through the mail.

It was vaporware.

Back in those heady, tech-bubble days it was common to hear of companies promising some new "killer-app" that would become the Next Big Thing. There would be rumors and supposedly insider tips, and sometimes full-blown public hype. Maybe there would be a demo, or some screenshots. If it was a startup company there would be cool branding, a slick speech about how the software or website was going to be a "game changer." It was always "next gen" and based on a revolutionary model. It was in final development, it would be released very soon. If you were lucky, if you had the right contacts, you could get on the deal before everyone else.

It wasn't hardware, it wasn't software, it was "vaporware." There was no substance. Maybe it was a good idea that just didn't gel, or overly ambitious developers who couldn't pull off what they promised, or deluded dreamers who were better at selling than doing. Sometimes it was dishonest hucksters who hyped half-baked ideas to charm investors out of money. Whatever the reason, vaporware is an example of the old saying that, "If it sounds too good to be true, it probably is."

Vaporware is also a symbol of a certain something that runs deeply through Generation X. I'm not sure what it is, exactly. Optimism? Vision? Laziness? Gullibility? As a generation we are weirdly drawn to the idea that we can get rich quick by getting in on the ground floor of clever new business opportunities in entertainment or media or on the Internet. It's not hard to see why we're fascinated by this mythology. We grew up with these industries, and people like George Lucas, Bill Gates, and Sergey Brin and Larry Page (the founders of Google) are our modern Rockefellers and Carnegies. We've watched Apple and Amazon and Google change our world like Ford and Standard Oil changed the world at the turn of the twentieth century. A hundred years ago people fell for scams by buying drilling rights on worthless land or patents on inventions to run engines on tap water.

This type of mythology has a core belief: that wealth and success are just a result of having the right connections and getting some some lucky breaks. Some folks really do believe that the only thing standing between them and fame and fortune are contacts and an inside tip. They become hangers-on and groupies to people they think can get them into the right circles. They also buy into schemes that they think will help them to jump the line and get ahead of everyone else. They consider this to be a smarter path to success than hard work.

Most of us like to think that we're trailblazers, but we really aren't. Trailblazers are few and far between; that's why they're called trailblazers. Most of us just react and follow the herd, which is how bubbles markets form. In the late 1990s it was the dot-com bubble, with companies like Pets.com leading the charge. It seemed like everyone was day trading the NASDAQ and getting tips on hot IPO's. You felt kind of dumb and left out if you weren't buying tech stocks. After that was the housing bubble, when we all suffered the mass delusion that over-leveraged real estate values would rise forever. Back in the early 1980s there was an oil and gas investment bubble. It seems that every decade some industry has a run up, and we all chase after it. Some of us get excited when we hear about an opportunity that seems to offer a way to catch up with the lucky ones who got in on the ground floor. Too often we end up buying vaporware.

The vaporware fantasy isn't new. Remember Jack?

Jack was a lazy young man whose family was starving. In desperation, his mother sends him to the market one day to sell their last possession, a milk cow. She sits at home, worrying and waiting for him to complete the simple task and bring home some cash that could keep them alive.

Along the way, Jack meets a stranger who tells him that he seems like far too clever of a lad to be wasting his time with cow sales. The stranger has a unique product, not the kind of thing available to the general public. But the stranger says he likes Jack, so he'll let him in on a special deal: five magic beans for his cow. Jack hesitates, but in the end he's too sharp to miss out on an opportunity like this. He hands over the cow and rushes home to mom. She's eager to know how much he got for the cow, and when he tells her that he got an inside deal for five magic beans she cries out in double despair: they are doomed to starve and her son is plainly an idiot. She throws the beans out the window and goes to lay down and die from hunger and shame over her dolt of an offspring.

If the story of *Jack and the Beanstalk* stopped there, it would be a simple illustration of vaporware. But it's more interesting than that: the story doesn't condemn vaporware, but feeds the myth.

Because it turns out that mom doesn't know what she's talking about, and the beans really *are* magic. A giant beanstalk grows overnight, giving Jack a way into a castle in the sky. He sneaks into a giant's home, manipulates the giant's wife and burglarizes the place. He discovers that the giant is only rich because he has a golden singing harp and a goose that lays golden eggs. Jack steals them both and brings them home to mom. With the giant's loot they become wealthy, Jack gets to marry a princess and they all (except the giant and his wife) live happily ever after.

What, exactly, is the moral of this story? I'm not sure, but I guess it would be that we shouldn't listen to the naysayers: sometimes vaporware is the real deal. Get hooked up with the right people if you want to get into the big leagues. Everyone there is only there because they have some unfair advantage (waterfowl that drop precious metals out of their bottoms). You can get some of that action for yourself. Then you'll show mom and everyone else who called you a lazy idiot! You'll buy a big house and get a hot-looking trophy wife.

They may not have called it vaporware, but people have always been looking for shortcuts to success, and lots of them have fallen for schemes and scams.

On January 24, 1848, James Marshall was working on a lumber mill that he was building for John Sutter, a landowner and developer near Sacramento, California. He found some shiny metal fragments in a sluice that channeled the American River through the mill. Marshall brought them to Sutter and they had them tested. It didn't take long for word to leak out, and within a matter of weeks newspapers in San Francisco were proclaiming that the American River was full of gold.

Sutter's employees, and just about all the laborers in the area, abandoned their jobs to pan for gold. Soon, San Francisco itself became a ghost town as everyone rushed for the gold fields. The California Gold Rush was on.

Over the next few years hundreds of thousands of people came to California in search of gold. They became known as *Forty Niners,* since the bulk started arriving in 1849. The Forty Niners came from Latin America, China and just about everywhere else on Earth. Most came from the eastern United States, enduring at least a six-month journey by land or sea. They sold everything they had and risked it all on a life-changing gamble. The first ones to hit the gold fields made a profit, harvesting the easy-to-find nuggets. The later prospectors struggled to clear their expenses for the journey and supplies. In the end, the merchants who supplied the Forty Niners made most of the money. San Francisco became a world-class city, California became a state and the industries and infrastructures of the West Coast were built.

So what's so unique about Generation X's vaporware dreams? Weren't the Forty Niners chasing after get-rich schemes as well? Hasn't this been the American way, and hasn't it, mostly, worked out pretty well?

Yes, people have always raced for opportunities to get rich. That's human nature, and I can't blame anyone for that. During those wild days in the middle of the nineteenth century, showman and promoter P.T. Barnum said, "There's a sucker born every minute." But there are some important differences between Generation X and the Forty Niners. For one, the Forty Niners actually risked life, limb and everything they owned. It may have been wildly optimistic to believe that they could pick gold out of the rivers of California, and for most of them it may have turned out to be vaporware. But they threw themselves into and worked at it in ways that few Gen Xers can even imagine, much less emulate. Too many of us have the imagination of a Forty Niner without their courage or work ethic.

Why is our generation more vulnerable to schemes and scams in pursuit of vaporware fantasies? Like we've already seen in this book, we grew up during the Great Abundance, the longest economic expansion in American history. We grew up during a time when our material comforts were never really challenged. And we've grown up during a technological revolution that has changed human life, shrinking time and space. The total commitment and hardships that pioneers and risk takers endured throughout history are inconceivable to us.

It's important to acknowledge my own failure here, and my remorse. It made me feel clever to borrow money to buy businesses and to chase vaporware. It cost me, but I never risked what the entrepreneurs and pioneers of earlier generations risked. In the end, when my ventures didn't pan out, I walked into that bankruptcy court with my fill-in attorney, got my debts discharged, and walked out again. Not only was my life never in danger, the bankruptcy laws allowed me to keep my home and car (if I want to keep paying for them), and start over again with a slate that's not exactly clean, but hasn't kept me from moving on with a new business. I have friends who did the right thing: they managed their money well and didn't take wild chances. They still have mortgages and car payments. In filing bankruptcy out of my desperation, I did something I despise, and even find reprehensible.

Generation X grew up in a world where technology and a developed economy reward bright ideas and business acumen, but no one has to cross a continent in a covered wagon with their children to get ahead. Chasing a vaporware scheme doesn't get anyone killed or tossed in debtors' prison. Neither success nor failure costs as much as it did in the past. It's easier for us to believe in shortcuts and gamble on schemes.

I've been involved in a couple of multilevel marketing businesses over the years. I appreciate the intentions of many people who get involved in these operations. I've known hundreds of honest people who aspire to be self-employed. Many of them dream of owning a business, running it ethically and providing for their families. Their dreams are no different from the hundreds of thousands who heard about the gold in California or the Yukon, or the silver in Colorado and longed for a better life.

Dreaming about an opportunity, even reaching out for that dream, doesn't make it a sound investment. If the business model doesn't work, it doesn't work. If a family liquidated their life savings for the opportunity to pan for gold in a California river, that didn't mean that there would be any gold left by the time they got there. They may never have found enough nuggets to recoup their investment. Their life savings may have ended up mostly in the pockets of the wagon train operators and San Francisco merchants and the land speculators that sold them the rights to prospect on some piece of ground. In the same way, there may have been investors who spent the inheritance their grandmother left them to buy Pets.com stock. Their good intentions and ambitions couldn't turn vaporware into a solid business model.

I wonder whether the optimism I saw in people who came to the multilevel marketing meetings was always well placed. Too many times it felt like a Pets.com-type scenario: a bad business model, wrapped in hype, being sold to the hopeful. Of all the leaders who would talk about how successful they had become, I wish that I had met just one who didn't "get in" early and still actually made their money selling the "product" (be it energy drinks, toilet paper or domain names). In contrast, most of them made their money by selling the right to sell the "product" to the would-be entrepreneurs underneath them. Or they made their money by keeping people "in" through motivation and education.

There are honest-to-God good people in multilevel marketing who provide friendship, mentoring and a valuable experience to those who join their business. Sadly however, that value gets buried beneath expensive conferences, educational materials, weekly meetings, and constant pressure to "qualify" for certain associations and accolades by pushing a broken business model that lost most of its value shortly after it launched. In the end, you find a revolving door business and hundreds of people who are bitter and broke who will go out of their way to warn the rest of the public about you and your business. Vaporware.

The Internet has become our magic beans; because we grew up with it, or it with us, we believe in its infinite wonders. It's our gold fields, and like the Forty Niners some of us have boundless optimism that we can strike it rich on the Web. Some of us try to launch innovative businesses, but too many of us think that we can pan for gold online. It seems that everyday I see or get approached with one vaporware scheme or another. Many them are multilevel marketing or online based: there are no profitable products, and if there are you're one of thousands of people competing for the same few customers. In reality you're just buying the idea of a product from someone and selling it to someone else. The dream of web-based "passive income" is our version of Jack's golden-egg-laying goose.

One of the consequences of Generation X's endless series of online and multilevel business models is that we are becoming increasingly a service-based generation and a service-based economy.

Not enough of us actually create wealth, we just have projects and plans to manage, transfer or promote wealth. The problem with a service-based economy is that it just sloshes money around but doesn't generate it. A country where everyone just takes in each others' laundry is a poor country.

As much as Generation X is drawn to shortcuts, schemes and scams, fundamental economic realities cannot be ignored, or at least not for long. We can't sell things for less than they cost. We can't borrow money endlessly. We can't just sell the right to sell hype to other people, like a perpetual motion machine. Somehow, somewhere, someone has to make something of value and sell it for a legitimate profit or the whole economic house of cards will collapse. We have to learn that there are only so many people who can legitimately make money from one product being sold to one person. With our technological age, that number of people is getting smaller, which means we must create more and leverage less. For several years we have been doing the opposite. Good ideas, those that benefit humanity, must become a reality. We must align our thinking, our practice, and our politics around this objective.

Steve Jobs, the founder of Apple Computers has been accused of overhyping his products. Even if you're not an Apple fan you have to admit that Jobs hasn't built a career peddling vaporware. In 1983, during the final push to complete the design of the Macintosh computer, Jobs took his development team to an offsite retreat to brainstorm and figure out how to turn all their hard work into a finished product. They were behind schedule, and in danger of missing the promised shipping date for the first Macs. He issued an edict: "Real Artists Ship." He meant that good ideas and good intentions weren't enough. Great designers, great businessmen and great companies--like great artists--produce tangible results, not vaporware.

Generation X needs to lead America away from the mythology of magic beans and vaporware. Americans should never stop dreaming or being ambitious. It's our heritage and our birthright. Americans need to be people who produce things--great things--that make sense. We must commit to solid business models and practices. If we will accept nothing less than real products made by real companies for real profits, then America can once again become strong and solvent, and once again be a nation that the rest of the world looks to for example and assistance, instead of the other way around.

Chapter 6
"The Debt Star"

Have you ever been reminded of something you said, maybe years later, and been embarrassed that something like that could have ever come out of your mouth? That happened to me not too long ago. A friend reminded me of a conversation we had back in my wheeling-and-dealing days. I had just built myself an executive home, I was driving a luxury car, and I was in the process of buying all those residential properties to "flip." Apparently (I don't remember the conversation) I was encouraging my friend to buy himself a new, nicer home. He said that he didn't think that he could afford it, and asked how I was able to keep buying more stuff. He says I replied, "It's the magic of equity. Leverage your equity."

In hindsight, that's cringe-worthy.

A few years later I was sitting in a hearing room with my fill-in attorney, completing my personal bankruptcy. I had learned some bitter lessons. Back when I told my friend about the magic of equity, I thought that debt was the raw material from which clever entrepreneurs spun gold. It made me feel clever and worldly to talk to lenders and business partners on my cell phone as I drove my luxury car between meetings. I felt smarter than the average person who was content with their little paycheck. I thought of myself as an engine of economic growth, taking out lines of credit to pay off other credit lines, buying stuff and leveraging it against other stuff like gears and flywheels in some complicated machine. It seemed too good to be true as the machine's borrowing power just kept getting bigger.

Did I ever have doubts? Sure, but the bankers kept approving my loans. Whenever I wondered whether I was in too deep I took comfort in their complicity and my ever-increasing appraised real estate values. Whenever I applied for a new loan they looked over the files and approved it. I figured that they must know what they were doing, and that they were conducting their "due diligence." If they were comfortable risking their banks assets on me and my assets, then I figured that I must be doing something right. Somewhere up the food chain, the grown-ups must have been checking all this out and they kept on giving me green lights. So I didn't worry too much about it.

Yeah, I know: cringe-worthy.

Ever since the banking system began melting down in 2008 we have been making one horrifying discovery after another, which add up to this: there are no grown-ups in charge. There is no wise, benevolent grandfather type, some sort of Wilford Brimley character, who is managing the family estate, keeping it solvent for us unruly kids. We are squandering the family fortune and no one is going to stop us or has a plan to save the ancestral farm.

Like the Death Star in *Star Wars*, America's debt is ominous and threatens our way of life. Our private and public indebtedness (more on that distinction in a bit) has gotten so big, and so out of control, that it has become a malignant force that can't be ignored anymore. It's like one of those Guinness-Book-of-World-Record cases where someone has a tumor the size of a basketball removed and you wonder, "How could they have just let that grow inside of them for ten years?".

Just to spoil your day, Google or Yahoo or Bing (however you search) the phrase "debt clock real time." There are a number of sites hosting this little shop of horrors. I found it at *www.usdebtclock.org.* The screen is full of little windows with continuously updating numbers. One section shows our income: U.S. Gross Domestic Product (GDP), breakdowns of that by citizen and worker and how much tax revenue is being collected by the federal and state governments. Those numbers are green. Other sections list our current debts, calculated in real-time, and those numbers are red. Take a look at total *public* (government) debt, broken down per citizen and per taxpayer (as I sit here those numbers are $39,412 and $111,483). It gives us real-time updates on our *private* debts, what citizens owe for mortgages, car loans, credit cards and the like. Right now, it lists the private debt per citizen as $54,167. The bottom section lists our assets, business and personal, in green. Currently we have $256,257 in assets per citizen, but we have $346,260 (red numbers) in unfunded liabilities per citizen (things like Social Security, prescription drugs, Medicare, etc.).

It's not just the United States, either. I just looked at a map online from the *CIA World Factbook* (great statistical resource, by the way). America's national debt is listed at 60.8% of GDP. That means that our standing debt is about 61% of our annual income as a nation. It would be like a family with a $100,000 income having $61,000 in debt. The other industrial nations with comparable lifestyles and values have similar debt loads: Canada, France, Germany and the UK all have debt loads in the 50-70% of GDP range. The concern is where we're all going: if our GDP doesn't grow as fast as our debt loads, we're going to creep above the 70% line. What does that look like? This map shows that Italy has crossed over the 100% threshold: its debt is 103.7% of GDP. Japan is even worse with a national debt that's a staggering 170.4% of their gross domestic product. It's hard to imagine how countries like that can ever grow their income enough to pay that down. A huge portion of their public revenue just goes to paying interest on their public debt.

Our debt clock isn't slowing down, and there's no reason to think it's going to. What starts as an annoyance becomes a burden, and then an unbearable burden. Ultimately, our Debt Star threatens to end the Great Abundance we grew up in. We've bought so much stuff and agreed to so many things that we can't earn enough as a nation to keep up with it. Eventually those commitments eat into our ability to have other things. Interest on debt at all levels, public and personal, take more out of every dollar we have to spend. Our choices become more limited. Publicly we can't have the same roads, schools, healthcare or military that we grew up with. Privately, we face the very real possibility that we won't do as well as our parents. Into our forties many of us still need to get loans and help from our baby boomer parents or "greatest generation" grandparents. Will we still be doing that into our fifties? Our sixties? Most of my friends are starting to realize that we will never retire like our parents did, and the Social Security and other benefits they enjoy will be long gone before it's our turn to use them.

I think that we're right to be angry at the Baby-Boom generation for sticking us with the public (government) debt we've got. It was their votes and their leadership over the last twenty plus years that built the Debt Star. But much of the private debt is our own fault: no one forced me to buy those cars or houses. It's hard to blame our credit card bills on someone else. We may feel, like I did, that the bankers and finance companies should have cut us off if they saw us getting in too deep. After all, if we were out of control, weren't they concerned about getting repaid? Shouldn't they have, you know, checked us out or something? That's a weird excuse, though. It's as if you returned a rental car all busted up and said to the rental company, "Well, it's your own fault for not screening me better. If you really cared about your car you never should have lent it to me in the first place."

Here's another sobering thought: our private debt is being socialized, or rolled into our public debt through government bail outs. All those bad loans to businesses and individuals are being wrapped up into public liabilities. It isn't just through bailouts either; more of us are relying on government support and subsidies because we can't make ends meet. To make matters worse, since we aren't as prosperous, the government collects less tax from us, creating even more public debt. The cycle is vicious and it's genuinely difficult to imagine any realistic solutions. We may very well be caught in a failure loop like Argentina was at the turn of the twentieth century. It went from being a prosperous, world-class nation to a basket case and has never really recovered.

How can Generation X defeat the Debt Star?

I'm not going to offer solutions to our public debt nightmare. Those solutions are, by definition, political decisions. America is going to have to balance its income (taxes) and expenses (all that stuff we want the government to give us). That isn't simple, for two reasons. First, taxation and national prosperity are linked. If we collected no taxes at all, people would have more cash, but society would disintegrate without roads, courts, schools, police, the military, etc. On the other hand, society would also disintegrate if the tax rate was 100%, meaning we took every penny people earned and the government spent it. Who would go to work? One of the reasons we have a democracy is so that we can argue about how, and how much, the government should collect and spend. Those arguments involve facts, values and political philosophies and I can't resolve them on these pages, so I'm not even going to wade into them.

I do want to talk about our private debt which, as I pointed out, is quickly becoming absorbed into our public debt. Remember how the Death Star was supposed to be invulnerable to a large-scale attack, but individual fighters could penetrate its defenses? Do you also remember how the Death Star was a gigantic, single-point-of-failure system? If an individual ship could score a direct hit on one particular exhaust port, the whole thing would blow up. Our Debt Star may be well-defended against a large-scale, public assault, but I think that it is vulnerable to individual attacks. Each of us can attack it at its greatest point of vulnerability.

Stop spending more than you make.

That's it, my brilliant solution. Each of us should stop borrowing so much money. I won't say stop borrowing altogether, because there are some cases (buying a house, capitalizing a business, getting an education) where it often makes sense. Even though some debt, sometimes, might make some sense, it should be the exception in our lives and not the rule. When we do take on debt, it should be as small as possible, and we should pay it off as quickly as we can. Debt should never be something that we take on in order to live beyond our means.

I just checked the debt clock again. At the moment it's telling me that the personal savings per adult in the United States is $2,738. Wow. I just jumped over to the U.S. Department of Commerce website and checked out a chart titled "Personal Savings Rate." It shows the "percentage of disposable income" saved by Americans since 2004. Over the last five years we have saved, on average, between one and three percent of our disposable income. However, in the second quarter of 2009 when it seemed the economy was evaporating in front of our eyes, the rate shot up to almost five percent before dropping back to three percent in the third quarter. In other words, when we got frightened enough, we doubled our savings rate, but we couldn't sustain it.

I found another chart from the Bureau of Economic Analysis, that says the U.S. personal savings rate was closer to eight percent in

1990, about the time that most of Generation X was getting out of college and starting careers. It has plummeted since then. I found another chart online from an economic think tank that showed the French and Germans saving something closer to ten percent of their annual income (and those are high-tax countries). Supposedly, the Chinese save somewhere between twenty and thirty percent of their paychecks.

What that tells me is that some people aren't just living within their means, they're actually living below their means. The math is simple: if you save ten percent of your disposable income, every ten months you have another month's income at your disposal. If you do that for five years, with interest you probably have more than six months living expenses set aside.

As I'm writing this in the winter of 2009 lots of us are hanging on by our fingernails, trying to keep a roof over our heads and food on the table. How do we save ten percent of our income when we're coming up more than ten percent short trying to pay the bills? Well, it's going to take serious lifestyle changes. We're going to have to control, if not cure, the consumer-driven affluenza that we grew up with. That's easy to say, like reminding each other that if we only ate less and exercised more we wouldn't be so fat. Like any lifestyle change it's hard to do. For it to "stick," we have to change our values, and maybe even our worldview. Are we willing to be secure with less, or would we rather have more but have it precariously?

I've written about my bankruptcy, but let me tell you about my life now. My wife and I live below our means. We use cash for most things. I drive a used car with lots of miles on it and we have downsized our house. We've become downwardly mobile. As a result, we are living on less than 25% of the income we had--and needed to have--when we were flying high. We can afford everything around us and are even able to give and save a little. We're happier than we've ever been. We don't worry like we used to. We sleep better at night. Life is getting better. Bankruptcy got me out of hot water; changing my life keeps me from going back into the pot.

What would be the cumulative effect if our generation started living, not like our parents, but like our grandparents? They lived through the Great Depression and World War II. It affected them permanently. They learned to live below their means, to be frugal and save. They built a prosperous country for their kids, our parents, who didn't have to learn those things. Our parents raised us during this era that some have called the Great Abundance, more than half a century of American economic expansion from the early 1950s until...well, now, maybe. I'm writing this in the midst of what is already the Great Recession and we're praying will not become a second Great Depression. If we learn and apply the personal lessons our grandparents did, might we find our way through this mess?

Have you ever heard the First Rule of Holes? It's this: when you're in one, stop digging. At the moment the banks have pulled back and are making it harder to get loans. That won't last long, since even our political leaders are pressuring them to start lending money again so that we can all get back to borrowing and buying. Each of us has control over his or her own actions, though. When the economy picks up a little bit again, and it will at some point, don't dig your hole deeper. Don't buy so much stuff and borrow so much money. Save at least ten percent of what you make. We need to stop believing that the

Great Abundance was our birthright, that we are entitled to making and spending more every year than we did the year before. We need to take responsibility for our own lives, not hope and expect that there are grown-ups somewhere who will fix our problems.

What will that do to our economy? America depends on consumption. We buy more things than we make, and if we all stop buying things what will happen to honest people who work in businesses that sell us our cars, clothes, computers and everything else?

I'm not a trained economist, but I think that common sense should tell us two things. First, we're not going to stop buying, or even borrowing, completely. I'm certainly not suggesting that we live in huts, weaving our clothes and making our own shoes. What I'm saying is that if we all lived slightly below our individual means we'd be healthier and happier. I can testify to that from personal experience. We'd also have something set aside for the proverbial rainy day. Some of us will still buy boats (if this book sells well enough maybe I'll even be one of them), but we will be able to afford them, maybe even pay cash for them instead of running up crushing debts for them. The second thing common sense tells me is that if our economy is based on all of us living beyond our means, borrowing to buy more than we can afford, then our economy is unsustainable. If that's the house of cards we've built then it's going to come down eventually and we might as well start changing it now. Honestly, I don't think it has to change as much as some of us fear. There could still be restaurants on every corner, but if we were more frugal maybe the prices would be a bit less. The portions would have to be smaller, too, but is that a bad thing?

The Debt Star can be destroyed if our culture changes. If we become a generation that spends less and saves more, I guarantee that we will be a generation that lives better.

Chapter 7
"Ship of Fools"

I'm not what you'd call an art history guy, but I saw a painting that really intrigued me. It's from an artist with the unusual name of Hieronymus Bosch, who lived in what we now call the Netherlands during the late fifteenth century. The painting is called *Ship of Fools,* and my Google-Fu reveals that Bosch created it sometime in the 1490s and that it hangs today in the Louvre museum in Paris.

Ship of Fools portrays a small boat, sailing in a sea that stretches out to the horizon, but with ominous looking cliffs off to one side. The boat is clearly adrift, without navigation or direction, because the people aboard are too busy partying. A monk and a nun are singing to each other while she plays a lute. They look like they're about to get it on. There's a fat guy at one end who looks stoned and appears to be dangling a wine jug over the side of the ship to hide it from a woman who's bonking him over the head with a pitcher. Three guys are standing around bobbing at what looks like a...I don't know, I guess it looks like a pancake, that's dangling from a rope. Don't ask me why. One of them looks like he's supposed to be steering, but the rudder has been replaced by a big spoon, and he's not paying attention to where they're going anyway. They could be drifting dangerously close to those rocky cliffs. Meanwhile, another dude next to a wine or beer cask is vomiting over the side. That, I do get. Two naked guys are swimming alongside the ship (I don't want to know), and one has a bowl he's holding up, hoping that someone will give him a refill (why not?).

The mast and sails have been replaced by three trees, and there's a fool (the court jester kind) sitting in one of them, who looks like he's a mellow drunk, sipping from his cup. Up top there's a roast goose tied to the top tree, and a guy is climbing up with a knife, trying to cut it down. Above him is a flag with the Islamic Crescent and above that, hiding in the upper branches, is what appears to be an owl.

What does all of this mean? I have absolutely no idea. I found some art history websites that interpret the symbolism in various ways, but no one seems to be in complete agreement. Bosch was, apparently, a surrealist, painting fantastic scenes that can be understood many ways.

So why do I bring it up? Because regardless of what Bosch was trying to say, *Ship of Fools* struck me as a perfect metaphor for Generation X. We are adrift, not knowing where we're going or how to get there. We are ridiculously consumed by our entertainments and amusements and parties. Our world is senseless, confusing and defies interpretation.

In fact, it's precisely because the meaning is obscure that *Ship of Fools* seems like such a good metaphor for our generation: we are consumed by absurdity, convinced that there is no higher meaning or purpose.

As a generation, we are obsessed with entertainment. I don't think it's a stretch to say that we don't value anything more than we do entertainment, entertainers and the entertainment industry. You might react by arguing that Gen X cares about social action and stuff like that. Well, sort of, but our high priests of social, global, ecological or whatever other kind of action are (wait for it)...entertainers. At least we came by that honestly: some of us first became aware of Africa by hearing all the Band Aid rock stars singing *Do They Know It's Christmas?* in 1984. The next year we learned that caring about starving people in Africa was cool when we watched Live Aid and watched even more hip, groovy and socially conscious rock stars swaying together on MTV, singing *We Are the World* at Live AID. This was followed by Farm AID, everything Bono has ever done, Rock the Vote and Al Gore's movie.

Music, movies and merchandise are the mediums through which we understand the world. We don't have bishops and popes anymore, we have stars: rock stars and movie stars tell us how much they care about issues and make it cool for us to care about them as well. We wear the ribbons and buy the social action T-shirts they wear. We show we care by going to awareness-raising concerts, seeing politically conscious movies, running cause-oriented 5k races with commemorative T-shirts and buying socially-branded products that donate a few pennies of the purchase price to some cause. This is how Gen X changes the world.

The common thread through all of us is our constant need to be entertained. Our generation's limited attention span--or our attention deficit disorder--makes it impossible for us to engage in any meaningful pursuit without it being properly branded and celebrity-endorsed. Of course, it also needs to be properly merchandised.

We invest more in our entertainment than any generation in history because it is so available. Earlier generations might have gone to stage plays or concerts, but those things were rare for most people. There were limits to how much of your life could be spent being passively entertained. No one, except for a few aristocrats living in big cities, could go to the opera every night. Of course the Greatest Generation grew up with radio, and their kids (the baby boomers) had broadcast television. But those devices weren't as omnipresent in their lives as cable TV, internet, video games, boom boxes, Walkmans, mall cineplexes, car audio, iPods and smart phones have been in ours.

The expansion of media entertainment into every waking minute of our lives isn't just the result of new technology. Entertainment grew to fill the space created by two other social trends in our lifetime.

First, lots of our moms went to work. Of course, women have always worked and some have always worked outside of the home. Yet during the 1970's-80's Baby Boom women began working outside the home to a degree unprecedented in American history. I'm not saying that it was wrong, or that there weren't a lot of good reasons for it, but the fact is that Gen X grew up with fewer moms at home than the generations before us. We also had fewer siblings: Gen Xers are sometimes called the Baby Busters because after the Baby Boom of the late 1940s and 50s birth rates plummeted in the 1960s and 70s. The baby boomers redefined the American ideas of work and family (indeed, they're proud of that accomplishment). They also divorced and geographically relocated away from family more than any previous American generation. The bottom line is that lots of Gen Xers grew up without being surrounded by family because mom worked, grandma and grandpa were in another city and we didn't have a house full of brothers and sisters. Entertainment filled the gap in our formative years: we were the first generation with cable TV, MTV & VH1, VCR's, video game consoles, Walkmans and the ability to make "mix tapes" for our car stereos. Being entertained, all the time, became the new normal.

There was another big change in American life that filled our days with ceaseless entertainment: our country moved indoors. Beginning in the 1970s the buildings that we spent our lives in got a lot bigger. Homes got more bedrooms, and that combined with fewer children meant that more children had their own rooms than in previous generations. The square footage swelled as the idea of the American home changed. People no longer lived in the neighborhoods that they grew up in. For a variety of reasons we became more mobile. We moved into housing developments where the architecture isolated us from our neighbors, who were strangers anyway. Front yards shrunk while backyards got walls around them, driveways got shorter and two car garages got closer to the street. We opened them with the new remote controls from inside our cars, and like a medieval lord and his entourage calling for the drawbridge to be lowered we pushed the button from halfway down the block, cruised inside and closed the garage door before exiting the vehicle. We unloaded groceries or whatever else and flipped on the cable TV, secure in our castle. Floor plans even invented new types of rooms: entertainment rooms, home theaters, game rooms.

The Great Indoors expanded everywhere we went. Schools got a lot bigger: compare a school built in the 50's or 60's with the mall-like structures of the 80's and 90's. Not only were they bigger, but they were full of rooms devoted to entertainment: performing arts centers, broadcast rooms, etc. Churches got huge, and sanctuaries were designed to be performing arts venues, with state of the art gear (helping to create those rooms was how I started making "big" money). Some children's ministry spaces got animatronic talking figures, just like a Chuck E. Cheese restaurant (which was another gift from the Boomers to their kids). The teenage ministry spaces were designed to resemble night clubs or recreation centers, with music videos blaring from monitors everywhere. Regional shopping malls started popping up everywhere. The malls were supposed to be our town squares, destinations full of fast food, game arcades and multiplex theaters.

The more the Great Indoors grew the less reason there was for us to venture into the Great Outdoors. We did fewer outdoor things (where we would be deprived of our electronic amusements) than any generation before us. Our environments were designed to entertain us all the time.

Did we ask for this? Not really: we were too young to ask. Just as our grandparents showered our parents with lifestyles that they assumed the Boomers wanted, our folks assumed that we wanted to be entertained every waking minute, and built us a world to provide it.

Is this what Kurt Cobain was reacting to with his Gen X anthem, *Smells Like Teen Spirit?* That song doesn't just feel angry, but confused and desperate too. In the same way that Jim Morrison and the Doors vocalized the teenage alienation of the baby boomers, Kurt Cobain and Nirvana captured Gen X's sense that the institutions of our childhood gave us nothing but amusement: *"Here we are now: Entertain Us!"*

Some art historians argue that Bosch's *Ship of Fools* is a commentary (or metaphor? Or spoof?) on the Church. Apparently, during Bosch's day artists sometimes described the Church as the "ship of salvation," carrying its passengers safely to heaven. They interpret the image to be a sarcastic response to that view.

I don't know what Bosch intended to satirize with it, but I do know that he couldn't have foreseen that it was the perfect metaphor for the World Wide Web.

The Internet is the greatest communication and educational tool the world has ever known. I was able to see and research Hieronymus Bosch and tell you about it only through the magic--and that's nearly what it is--of the Web. The Web has put at our fingertips all of mankind's aspirations, disciplines and accomplishments. From our smart phones we can scroll satellite photos of the entire globe, access the world's libraries and communicate with people of every tongue, tribe and nation. We can trade commodities in Shanghai, learn Urdu, read bills pending before Congress and get the local news in Ireland. We can track planes in the air, ships at sea and packages on trucks. We can get a masters' degree and find a curry take-out place in Sao Paolo.

Throughout the centuries people longed for, and killed for, this type of power and knowledge. We should be using it to surf Google Earth, learn about the geography and history of our planet while we master the hard sciences and gaze at imagery from the Hubble space telescope, all the while listening to digitized recordings of the pioneers of Jazz.

What do we do with all this power? We take quizzes on Facebook (*"Which Flintstones vitamin would you be?" "Which Partridge Family member would you be?" "Which Tetris shape would you be? The L-shape!"*). And, of course, we surf a lot of porn.

Is there anything wrong with Facebook and porn? I'll set that morality question aside for now, but let me be totally clear: I don't think that the government should restrict our access to the Web. That's our constitutional right, and I'd fight to defend it.

My point is that when we are given the opportunity to do anything with our free time (more than any other generation in history) and nearly omniscient access to the combined wisdom and knowledge of the ages (the Web), what we actually choose to do is to play games, post barely literate ramblings and masturbate. It's a complete waste of the freedoms that the Founding Fathers and technology gave us. We are unmasked: it reveals the truth of who we are when nobody's looking. Bosch's painting rings true: we are a *Ship of Fools*, drifting dangerously close to the rocks while the Islamic Crescent rises over our heads.

Baby boomers were notoriously immature (some of them still haven't grown up), but as a generation they largely moved out of their parents' houses. They went away to Vietnam or college or Woodstock or communes or followed the Grateful Dead for thirty years, but they were mad enough at their parents to turn their backs on them and independent enough to not move back in. Lots of Gen Xers never moved out. As a generation, we delayed growing up as long as possible. We weren't angry with with our parents about Vietnam or Watergate like they were with their folks. Chuck E. Cheese and the malls and the home theaters may have left us feeling empty, but we didn't hate them. So we tried to stretch our teenage years as far into our twenties as possible. Some of us stayed living at home, some us went on elaborate spring break trips to relieve the pressure of...well, whatever we felt pressured by. Girls went wild on spring break, and, true to our generational ethos, we recorded it and sold DVD's on cable TV.

Reality TV is the natural offspring of the Society of the Spectacle and the *Ship of Fools*. We've turned life into entertainment and entertainment into life. We've blurred all the lines. What's real, what's showbiz, what's merchandizing? Do we know anymore? Do we care?

Our generation has created an amoral world. Not an immoral world: that means a world with bad morals. Our fixation with entertainment, our short attention span for complex ethical discussions, our disbelief in universal spiritual laws, our disconnect with history and tradition have come together to create an amoral society: one where there are no morals, good or bad. As a generation we generally believe that all morality is a matter of private scruples, not something that should govern our collective actions.

So we are the *Ship of Fools.* America is drifting economically, socially, politically. Our place in the world and our future is uncertain. Our government is impotent, our debt is staggering, our institutions are corrupt, and our religious institutions are crumbling. Unless we take corrective actions we will, at best, drift wherever events take us and, at worse, break up on the rocks that are looming ever closer.

Yet like the characters in Bosch's painting we are too busy amusing ourselves to pay attention to what is really going on around us, let alone work together to effectively change anything. We are engrossed in activities on our laptops and smart phones that our grandfather would have had to join the Navy and go to a distant port to experience. We have no idea where we are, no idea where we're going and no leadership we all can respect. We don't even perceive ourselves as part of the same crew: we see ourselves as individuals with no collective responsibility to our country. We are either too busy to notice our peril or perhaps distrust each other too much to pay attention when someone looks up from their cup or toys to point it out. We Gen Xers needs to stop entertaining ourselves long enough to take responsibility for where America is going and how it's getting there.

Chapter 8
"Too Big to Fail"

Narvik. You probably don't know if it's a person, place or thing. I certainly didn't. It turns out that it's a place, a town actually. It's a town in Norway, to be precise.

Narvik, Norway is 150 miles north of the Arctic Circle. It's a port on the North Sea, where iron is loaded from Sweden's nearby ore fields. During World War II Hitler considered it such a critical ice-free port that in 1940 he rushed to seize it, and was met by British and Norwegian ships in one of the first great naval battles of that war. More than a dozen destroyers were sunk, and Narvik has had a prosperous tourist business ever since, with scuba divers exploring the wrecks at the bottom of the fjord.

Near the end of 2007 Narvik became a "canary in the coal mine," an ominous first casualty in the global financial meltdown that came into full bloom a year later and is still affecting us at the beginning of 2010.

Near the end of 2007 it became clear that the city government of Narvik had lost something like a quarter or a half of its annual revenue. Not because of declining shipping or tourism, but because city government had invested a significant amount of its cash. Those investments tanked, badly. The town of 18,000 was facing drastic cuts in every kind of government service and missed a payroll for the first time. The Norwegian government said it wouldn't bail out the town, and the town faced the prospect of large loans to keep operating, at precisely the moment the international banking system was approaching collapse.

What, you might ask, did these fjord-dwellers invest in? Reindeer farms? Herring futures? A chain of Swedish meatball franchises with snowmobile drive-through windows?

Nope, the truth is even weirder: they bet the town on mortgages of stucco houses in California and Florida. Weirder yet, they didn't know that.

Do you remember hearing about all those bundles of bad mortgages that were sold up the food chain as better than gold? They were considered a sure thing because *as everyone knows* real estate, especially in places like California, Las Vegas, Phoenix and Florida, *always goes up.* Of course you remember "house flipping." As the junk mortgages were bundled the investment banks insured them from risk with "credit default swaps" just so that they would be extra safe.

All these super-shrewd "financial products" weren't just sold around Wall Street, they were aggressively marketed across the globe. In 2004 the little town of Narvik, Norway bought almost $45 million of these products from Citigroup through a Scandinavian financial services company. They weren't sold as bundled mortgages from the U.S. Sunbelt; they were vaguely understood but highly recommended "financial products." By the fall of 2007 the real estate market in the U.S. was already starting to collapse, and the people of Narvik watched their town's wealth evaporate.

Should the city council (or whatever they call city councils in Norway) have paid closer attention to what they were investing in? Absolutely, although they trusted the Norwegian brokers who trusted Citigroup who trusted the regional banks who trusted...well, you get the idea. The system disintegrated and millions of individuals and institutions across the globe saw their savings wiped out. As these Narviks (I'm henceforth coining a new word) faced individual ruin, by the end of 2008 Citigroup was deemed too big to fail, and started getting bailouts by the United States government. In June of 2009 Citigroup was removed from the New York Stock Exchange because so much of it was owned by the U.S. Government (taxpayers) that it wasn't really a tradable private company anymore.

The story of Narvik, Citigroup and the little pink houses in Ft. Lauderdale is like an Aesop Fable: we can draw all sorts of moral lessons from it. Economists will still be arguing about what happened and why it happened fifty years from now. In this chapter, though, let's consider one question: have our institutions (business, government, schools, churches, etc.) gotten too big? Are they not only too big to fail, but too big to succeed? Are they too big for us to understand and relate to? Are they too big to control?

Let me be totally clear: sometimes bigger is better. The reason that we enjoy so many wonderful technologies today, from vaccines to vacuum cleaners, is because of "economies of scale." If every doctor had to mix his own medicines or every school had to write its own curriculum, almost everything around us would be more expensive and of lower quality. It's just more efficient when large numbers of people work together to make something or solve some problem. It's generally a good thing when organizations combine efforts to standardize processes or combine their purchasing power or share overhead costs.

As we've seen in previous chapters, within Generation X's lifetime, technology has accelerated trends already at work. Take a simple example: filling out forms. When we collected data from people (sales orders, school registrations, medical history, etc.) on paper, there were limits to how efficient we could be. The forms were collected and organized in something called "paper files" in large boxes called "file cabinets" (I know this is hard to imagine, but stay with me). All this hardcopy data storage made it harder to share and compare information, especially since different organizations had different forms and formats. In our lifetimes technology made it possible to enter the data from forms into big databases, and then to directly input the information into networked or web-based systems. Information can be shared and compared and used in ways that make our lives better and easier. Most of us can barely remember a time when you couldn't send a package overnight and track its progress, or when you couldn't go to any ATM anywhere in the world to get cash, or for that matter use your credit card to buy gas from a self-serve station anytime of day, anywhere. These conveniences only came because organizations and systems got large enough to become efficient.

Still, efficiency comes at a cost. Chain retailers offer higher quality at lower cost because they buy in bulk, standardize processes, and share overhead costs. They don't have daily interaction with their community like a mom-and-pop shop does. A large university can offer more choices of programs and facilities, but students don't get to know their professors. Big governments can write big checks, but they don't respond to local voters.

Generation X must wrestle with a fundamental choice: what are we willing to trade for efficiency? How big do we want our merchants, our schools, our churches and our government to be? Of course we want to have our cake and eat it, too: we want homey, local institutions that offer all the advantages of big, efficient organizations. That isn't one of our choices.

We have to avoid magical thinking about what we want. If we shop at the corner mom-and-pop store we're not going to get all the choices and prices we do at WalMart or Amazon. Giving parents a choice of which school they send their children to means that some families will make different choices than we would. Going to a large church means larger facilities, staff and programs but less intimacy, and the pastor might not know your name. If we shrink the size of government we will be more free but will also have to do a better job taking care of ourselves and our neighbors.

The issue is, I think, one of scale. Of course we all have different tolerances and comfort zones: some people prefer big cities, big malls, big schools and some don't. Things can get so big that they are out of scale for normal, human interaction. Are our communities and organizations and institutions of a size that "works" for us? Do we understand them? Can we relate to them? Can we determine when they are telling the truth, or how well they are performing? Do they respond to us? Can we control them when they do wrong?

Is that part of what went wrong in Narvik? The town leaders there were neither uneducated nor stupid, but they were doing business with an investment system that was so big that no one, anywhere in the world, really understood it or could see all its parts. A local broker sold someone a mortgage on a three-bedroom tract home in Las Vegas. Neither of them knew that the mortgage was sold repeatedly through a system of investment banks, bundled into securities at each step along the way, until it ended up as a drop in the vast sea that was Citigroup on Wall Street. Investment banks that controlled assets as large as some countries sliced and diced and recombined parts of these mortgage bundles into security investment products. Then these were sold and resold through various financial services firms around the world, which eventually ended up as a part of a portfolio for the firefighters and teachers of Narvik. No one in the fjord had any idea that they were now the proud owners of a note on a ranch house on a cul-de-sac off a freeway twenty-five minutes off the Vegas Strip; nor that their city had bet its future on the fact that the couple who bought that house would stay married, keep their jobs, and make their monthly balloon payments. In the dozens (?) of transaction layers between Las Vegas and Narvik there was no one who fully understood the connections or could really assess the risk of the system.

That's what I mean by saying that, despite our different preferences for big cities or small towns, some institutions no longer operate at a human scale. The idea that a consumer can make rational decisions about how to invest his or her money presumes that we have some means to evaluate these products and the dozens of global actors involved in selling or managing them.

As I write this we are all being carried along in a global recession driven by financial and governmental systems that no one completely understands or can manage. We are asked to give an opinion about health-insurance reform plans involving behemoth government bureaucracies, insurance companies, managed health care organizations and hundreds of incalculable variables over the next ten years. How do we make informed decisions when all of this is at a scale that no one can fully comprehend?

Our generation will need to decide whether we want institutions that are scaled to ordinary human life. In some cases that might mean we reform them from the top down. We might decide, for example, to prohibit multinational, multilevel, investment marketing schemes like the one that nearly dismantled the world economy in 2007 – 2008. In some instances we may need to protest and push back against the growth and intrusion of government agencies into our lives. We may need to build organizations and institutions that work for us, like relying more on local government and organizations than federal ones. Most of the time it will involve each of us making personal lifestyle choices, like where we will shop, work, and worship.

Consider the scale of our business dealings. Each of us should be free to decide how to earn and spend our money. We can work for a large corporation or government agency; or we can work for, or start, a small business. America needs to safeguard those options and not make either of those choices difficult by imposing laws or taxes that limit businesses at either end of the scale. As consumers we need to protect the freedom of the marketplace to innovate and offer us what we want. We must resist the temptation to use government to limit the marketplace by squeezing mom-and-pops off of main street or burdening the WalMarts of the world so they can no longer offer the choices and prices they deliver best. Sometimes big and small businesses can innovate together to offer us the best of both worlds. For example, big, efficient restaurant supply companies make it easier for family owned restaurants to keep their inventories low and order just in time at low prices.

It would be great if we could bring those same kind of choices to our schools. Our public schools are increasingly driven by mandates from distant bureaucracies rather than by local concerns. State and federal mandates create a one-size-fits-all educational model that doesn't respond to individual families. Why shouldn't parents be free to send their kids to a school that emphasizes science and math, or the arts, or has uniforms or year-round classes? Parents get frustrated when their opportunity for input is minimal and policies are set by distant agencies and judges influenced by professional lobbyists. Schools that function on a human scale would be locally driven and would involve more choices through charters and vouchers.

In a couple chapters we're going to explore Alexis de Tocqueville's observations of America in the 1830s. He argued that Americans would resist Europe's mistakes at both ends of the political spectrum. America had a central government, language and culture that would prevent the sort of regional, almost tribal, conflict so common in other parts of the world. On the other hand, Americans actively participated in strong local governments that responded to the input of their citizens. The genius of the Constitution and American culture was that it balanced the scale of its operations: the federal government handled military and foreign issues, while local institutions responded to their constituents.

The paradox behind all of this is that the bigger institutions get, the less likely they will fail, but the more devastating it is if they do. In the last few decades all the organizations around us have become gargantuan. That has brought us many benefits, but some of them have grown into monsters we can no longer recognize, understand, or control. Now we're afraid that they're too big to fail and so we let the broken monsters stumble along, without a clue how to fix them and afraid of what would happen if we let them collapse.

I believe that if we think something is too big to fail all we are doing is delaying its failure. Failure is a necessary part of life and the marketplace. Natural selection teaches us that competition is necessary for growth and innovation. When we interfere with the competition between people, organizations or institutions we only perpetuate weakness or dysfunction.

That sounds heartless. What about compassion and mercy? What about second chances and giving people and institutions an opportunity to learn and grow? Isn't that what I did through my bankruptcy?

Absolutely. There is always a place for mercy and grace. We're not talking about the small and powerless and weak, we're talking about gigantic, unwieldy, unresponsive organizations that are so big they are no longer transparent or controllable. Organizations like that aren't victims and they don't need mercy. They need to restructure so that they are smaller and more competitive.

I like the slogan *fail often, fail fast, and fail cheap.* If we aren't failing regularly, we aren't trying. When we do fail, we need to do it quickly, learn our lessons and start trying to be successful again. When we operate at a manageable scale we can afford to fail cheaply, without taking down a town on a Norwegian fjord with us.

In a previous chapter I said that I had not had the opportunity to learn experience in the same way my pioneer ancestors in Holland, Michigan had. That's not exactly true. I had the twenty-first century equivalent to their experience. In the 1840s they might have had a cabin burn down through carelessness, or had a weak harvest because of poor farming techniques, or lost a child to cold, accident or disease. Those were the critical lessons that taught them how to make a life and build a town in a new land.

I learned those types of critical lessons through my failures and bankruptcy. The pioneers went through the equivalent of bankruptcy often through all sorts of hardships. I suspect that within the next few decades many us will learn tough lessons. When we empower ourselves to fail often, fail fast and fail cheap we unleash ourselves to experiment and invent a new way of life, like pioneers in a technological, global wilderness.

Chapter 9
"Losing the Horizon"

Small planes and my family do not get along. My family has had its share of incidents with small planes, including the tragic loss of my uncle as a result of a crash a few years ago. I've grown to have a healthy —shall we say "concern?"—for the things that can go wrong in a small plane. Of all of those, perhaps the most dangerous is when the pilot "loses the horizon."

A pilot loses the horizon when he no longer has any visual reference points, and can't tell whether the aircraft is level or not. You would think that a pilot could just feel that the plane is pitching or rolling, but centrifugal force and the inner ear can work to create something called "spatial disorientation." The aircraft can be pitching down toward the ground at a 45° angle, or rolling onto its side, or stalling, and a spatially disoriented pilot can't tell. This is especially likely at night or in heavy fog. Pilots sometimes call it flying in a black hole. The only anecdote is for the pilot to use his cockpit instruments, like the artificial horizon or pitch and roll indicator, and to trust them. A visually disoriented pilot who has lost the horizon sometimes has difficulty trusting the instruments because his inner ear and brain are telling him something else. If he cannot reorient and fly by the instrument readings, he can usually measure his life expectancy in minutes.

America has lost the horizon: we no longer have any reference points to know whether we are flying straight and level. Generation X must take the controls and reorient our society. Previous societies oriented themselves with lessons from experience (history) and moral and ethical standards. We have lost those references. We've become *ahistorical* and *amoral.*

Big disclaimer: you think that you know what I'm going to say, but you probably really don't. I'm not going to argue that America was a Christian nation and that only overt and public religiosity can return us to our greatness. I am a Christian, and I do think that it would be a good thing if more people were as well. But my point is *not* going to be that we are an immoral nation that needs revival.

Instead, I think that we have become *amoral.* We have also become *ahistorical.* The two are linked. I'm not sure if one causes the other, but they definitely reinforce each other. We haven't just lost the horizon. Our situation is far more precarious: we don't *know* that we've lost the horizon. We no longer believe the horizon matters, or that there even is one.

Let's start with morality. Most of us grew up thinking of morality as a restraint on our freedom. We just want to exercise our personal liberty but some religious busybodies stick their noses into our life and tell us what we can't do with our bodies or our money.

The American Founding Fathers, the guys who wrote the Constitution that guaranteed us that liberty, predicted that the whole system would break down unless we had a shared sense of morality. John Adams, who had as much to do with the Declaration of Independence and the creation of the United States as anyone, said that, "Our Constitution was made only for a moral and religious people. It is wholly inadequate to the government of any other." Freedom without morality is anarchy. While Religious freedom was of great importance to our founding fathers, a common (perhaps common sense) moral foundation was recognized as equally essential. They knew that a republic, and a free-market society, could not survive unless the people embraced a common moral foundation.

Here's a simple example that was in the news as I was writing this chapter. In October 2009 the *New York Times* reported that in France the public bicycle rental program was in real trouble. It was a great idea, exactly the kind of cooperative, green program that Generation Xers love and want to see all over the United States. There are coin and credit-cart operated bike racks all over downtown Paris.

In the racks are heavy duty and high quality cruiser bicycles, perfect for navigating the narrow and busy streets. Instead of using a taxi or even the Metro subway, people are encouraged to drop one euro in the vending machine (or swipe a card) that automatically releases one of the bikes from the rack. One can then ride the bike on whatever errands he has and simply return it within thirty minutes to any of the other rack machines in central Paris. If you go past thirty minutes the computer simply adds a small overage charge, like in a parking garage. Simple, elegant, beautiful. Over the last few years the bikes and the racks have become iconic in Paris, a symbol of the green urban movement.

You see the problem coming, don't you? According to the *New York Times* story, the custom-made bikes, which cost $3,500 each, are being stolen and resold in black markets in Eastern Europe or northern Africa. Others are being stolen for joy rides and left broken and stripped in alleys and ditches. According to the Times, 80 percent of the initial 20,000 bikes have been stolen or damaged. Now the Paris government has had to hire hundreds of workers just to fix the bikes to keep the program running. Not only has it been a budgetary failure, it has shaken Parisians' confidence in the concept of urban cooperation in carbon-reduction programs. The French paper *Le Monde* wrote that "The symbol of a fixed-up, eco-friendly city has become a new source for criminality...[the program] was aimed at civilizing city travel. It has increased incivilities."

Our generation wants to believe in things like the Paris bicycle program. We want to believe that we don't need religion, rules or restraints. We want to believe that, left to ourselves, we would not only get along with our neighbors, we would work with them for the common good.

Without knowing it, we have been influenced by another Frenchman who argued that it was organized society itself, with all of its rules and divisions, that breeds inequality and conflict. Jean Jacques Rousseau was a political philosopher who lived just before the American and French revolutions in the eighteenth century. Rousseau believed that primitive peoples, uncorrupted by our greed and selfishness, live in a state of natural harmony between each other and their environment. If we could only shed ourselves of organized religion, government and capitalism we would enjoy true freedom in that "state of nature." In his 1754 *Discourse on Inequality* Rousseau wrote:

> *The first man who, having fenced in a piece of land, said "This is mine," and found people naive enough to believe him, that man was the true founder of civil society. From how many crimes, wars, and murders, from how many horrors and misfortunes might not any one have saved mankind, by pulling up the stakes, or filling up the ditch, and crying to his fellows: Beware of listening to this impostor; you are undone if you once forget that the fruits of the earth belong to us all, and the earth itself to nobody.*

Not even Rousseau thought that in the ideal "state of nature" we would have morals. We wouldn't need them. We would be like chimpanzees or dolphins, interacting simply and innocently with each other and our environment according to the whims of our stomachs and our glands.

Even if we have never have heard of Jean Jacques Rousseau, lots of us agree with him. It's not that we're immoral, that we like to do bad things. Instead, we've become amoral: we don't think that anything is really bad except the constraints and constructs of society. We suspect that Judeo-Christian morality has caused more trouble than it's worth. We want to live as close to the ideal state of nature as possible. We're convinced that if we could, we would have a more peaceful, just and carbon-neutral world. We pin our hopes for solving twenty-first century problems on innovative solutions like the Paris bicycle rental program.

The hippies of the 1960s and 1970s probably loved Rousseau. They imagined that if we would all get natural, live close to the land and practice free love without too many possessions and rules, we'd be naked and happy all the time. The whole Woodstock generation experiment didn't turn out like most of them thought. Many Gen Xers hate corporations, protest the World Trade Organization and want to reject the materialism and greed we see around us. We fantasize about an eco-friendly, post-American, post-capitalist world where everyone would be, in the words of Bill and Ted, "Excellent to each other!"

I remember reading *Lord of the Flies* in school. Wait, hold on, that's a lie: I watched the movie and then read about it on *Wikipedia*. Anyway, lots of my friends tell me that they had to read it in high school. Written by William Golding in 1954, it imagines what would happen to a bunch of English schoolboys if they were shipwrecked alone on a deserted island. They hunt, fish and gather tropical fruit.

They also descend into anarchy. The word means "rule by no one," or "the absence of rulers."

In practice, anarchy isn't the absence of rules or government, or at least not for very long. It quickly becomes simply rule by the strongest and most violent, because in the absence of any moral restraint, the strong take from the weak.

That's why our French friend (who we'll discuss more in the next chapter), Alexis de Tocqueville, wrote, "Liberty cannot be established without morality, nor morality without faith." De Tocqueville's family had to flee from France into exile to escape the terror of the French Revolution, during which Rousseau's ideas were tested. The motto of that revolution, *liberté, égalité, fraternité* (Liberty, Equality and Brotherhood) descended into the guillotines of the Reign of Terror and the dictatorship of Napoleon Bonaparte.

To avoid anarchy and fascism a society must agree to some shared moral landmarks. There must be some things that everyone agrees are absolutely right and wrong. Our society doesn't necessarily delight in immorality, but our list of moral absolutes is short and growing shorter everyday. The idea of moral absolutes turns us off. That's one of the reasons why moderate Muslims reject western culture. While I may not share their religion, it does give them ethical landmarks. They look at us and see a landscape of moral anarchy.

Eighty percent of those high-quality, progressive bikes in Paris have been vandalized or stolen. What will happen to the rest of our brilliant, green, cooperative solutions if we don't have any moral principles to direct or restrain us? How will things like public health care, public housing, carbon credit systems or developing-world debt-relief plans play out in an amoral society? We don't need to speculate about that. Most of those things have been tried, and most of them have been as unsuccessful as the Paris bike program.

We have lost the horizon and are flying blind.

I'm not sure if it's a cause or effect, but I think our amorality is at least partially linked to us being ahistorical.

Everyone, and every group, believes some story about themselves. That story shapes who they are and how they behave. Some of us believe America was an evangelical, Christian country of simple individualistic virtues, and we look at our past, present and future through that lens. It fuels our patriotism and gives us a sense of loss. Some of us argue that America was, from the beginning, an imperialistic, genocidal, racist and oppressive oligarchy. That story doesn't cultivate patriotism or even loyalty. Those who hold those views are not necessarily unhappy to see America being taken down a few pegs in the world.

What is positive about both those stories is that they *are* stories. In other words, whichever narrative you subscribe to, you do have some historical reference that shapes your view of America's present or future. We then can have a vigorous argument, maybe even an old-fashioned shouting match, about which of those stories is true. You'll lay out your version of history, cite your sources, marshall your facts, bring forth your experts. I'll do the same, and then we'll keep on arguing about the accuracy and interpretation of our data. That's how it's supposed to work in a democracy. We may not all be convinced about everything, but hopefully we'll come to some consensus about a few points that can serve as our historical landmarks.

Most of us can't have that sort of intellectual bar fight because we don't know enough about history to argue about it. As I've said over and over, our obsession with the media-fed, pop-culture spectacle leaves us with little interest or energy to spend on old names, dates and events. Ask most Gen Xers about history and they'll roll their eyes. It's boring. Who cares? The History Channel on cable TV used to run entertaining but serious programs about history. While writing this I just popped over to their website and checked their list of "Most Watched" programs. In the top ten were: history of Bigfoot, the prophecies of Nostradamus, the mysteries of the Bermuda Triangle, something about Hercules, Giant Squid Attack, Capturing Hogzilla, something about meteorites or asteroids hitting the earth and "Gangs and Graffiti: the Story Behind the Images." I don't blame the History Channel, they're in business to put on programming that attracts viewers and apparently this is what does it.

Any serious discussions about America's economic, cultural, technological or foreign policy challenges must be calibrated by some understanding of our story. How did these problems arise? Why? Have we ever faced anything like this before? What did we do then? Did it work? I fully recognize that any of these questions might have multiple answers from a variety of perspectives. Yet if we tossed all those possible answers onto the table we could at least have a somewhat intelligent argument about them. Most of us can't do that today. We've become ahistorical in the sense that we don't know our own "backstory," or the backstory of the other players in our early, twenty-first century drama. Of course, if the discussion is going to revolve around whether Nostradamus predicted Bigfoot's gang tattoos, we're locked and loaded.

People like to quote George Santanyana, who said, "Those who cannot remember the past are condemned to repeat it." I prefer this one by the Roman politician Cicero, "He who knows only his own generation remains always a child." (Which a friend tells me is carved over the entrance to the library at the University of Colorado in Boulder.) We are perpetual children who think that our problems are unique. We have no sense that previous generations have struggled with similar problems. Sometimes they solved them, sometimes they didn't, and sometimes they kicked the can down the road for their great-grandchildren. Yet we flail about, trying to reinvent the wheel.

The root of this, I think, is another word that starts with "A:" apathy. Pathos is the Greek word for emotion, what we call passion. Apathy is a lack of passion. We are amoral and ahistorical because we have no passion about morality or history. We are children of the Great Abundance, growing up in a society that always got bigger, richer and more entertaining. We just haven't cared about anything else.

Amoral, ahistorical, and apathetic: we've lost the horizon. Now, as we try to figure out how to navigate through deep changes in our world, we are flying blind.

Chapter 10
"Freedom Fries, Davy Crockett and the Nanny State"

It was lame. There's no other word for it. Back in 2003, during the run-up to the Iraq War and France was vocally opposing the invasion in the United Nations, some pro-war restaurant owners thought a clever way to show their disgust with the "cheese-eating surrender monkeys" would be to remove "French Fries" and "French Toast" from their menus. Ah, you point out, call them what you want, but people *like* fried potatoes and egg-battered bread. Indeed. So they kept those on the menu but wittily renamed them "Freedom Fries" and "Freedom Toast." See, by using the word freedom they were making the point that Americans like freedom, unlike French people, who like...frying, or something. Get it? Clever, huh?

Anyway, even the U.S. Congress attempted to liberate our lunches from repressive, Gallic influence. On Capitol Hill the House cafeterias were ordered, henceforth, to only sell Freedom Fries and Freedom Toast. The company that makes French's Mustard was alarmed enough to issue a press-statement, swearing that their brand merely referred to the family name of the founder, and pointing out that their mustard loved democracy far more than their suspicious-sounding competitor, Grey Poupon (I wouldn't be surprised if all makers of Dijon mustards got surprise IRS audits). Supposedly, the spokeswoman for the French Embassy in Washington wrinkled her arrogant, little, continental nose and pointed out that *frites* probably came from Belgium, anyway--no doubt in an outrageous French accent.

So it's ironic that to understand the American idea of freedom and what's happening to it we turn to...a Frenchman.

Alexis de Tocqueville was born in 1805, 16 years after the rise of Napoleon Bonaparte. He came from an old, aristocratic family that had been exiled to England during the terror of the French Revolution, and in his twenties he began a career in politics. When he was 25 the French government sent him to America to study the American legal system; and he spent most of 1831 traveling extensively across the United States and Canada (such as they were then). De Tocqueville didn't confine himself to major cities but visited the frontier as well; sometimes bumping along in the back of mail carts to log-cabin communities deep in untamed forests, interviewing the pioneers he met. When he returned to France he published *Democracy in America,* a book that two hundred years later is still insightful and important.

One reason why de Tocqueville's analysis is so valuable is precisely because he was French. He brought an outsider's perspective, but more than that, he grasped the different influences that shaped the European countries (particularly the French) and America into such different types of nations.

This point is often lost when Americans argue for or against the way Europeans do things, whether it be government, education, health care, etc. France and America have been shaped by centuries of different events, cultures and patterns of development. On the surface we are a lot alike, but those influences made us into very different societies. The genius of de Tocqueville is that he spotted these important differences when they were in their infancy. He foresaw how we would grow up into very different peoples, particularly when it comes to our ideas about freedom and the individual's relationship to the government.

In *Democracy in America,* Alexis de Tocqueville notes that while there may be Americans who are poor, *"The Americans never use the word peasant."* He meant that America didn't have categories left over from thousands of years of class-stratified society in which even literacy and political participation were systematically withheld from the laboring masses. He continues, "They have no idea of the class which that term denotes; the ignorance of more remote ages, the simplicity of rural life, and the rusticity of the villager have not been preserved among them." Not only that, but he noted that even the culture of European village life was an alien concept to Americans. "They are alike unacquainted with the virtues, the vices, the coarse habits, and the simple graces of an early stage of civilization."

De Tocqueville argued that Americans didn't understand these things because the experience of taming the frontier and building a nation never allowed the rhythms and rules of European life to take hold. This was in spite of the fact that Americans in the wilderness often lived in worse conditions than peasants in a European village.

> *At the extreme borders of the confederated states, upon the confines of society and the wilderness, a population of bold adventurers have taken up their abode, who pierce the solitudes of the American woods and seek a country there in order to escape the poverty that awaited them in their native home. As soon as the pioneer reaches the place which is to serve him for a retreat, he fells a few trees and builds a log house. Nothing can offer a more miserable aspect than these isolated dwellings.*

Yet unlike so many Europeans who had been bred into their place and position in the world through dozens of generations, each generation of Americans invented themselves anew. The frontier, which was ever-moving west from the day the Mayflower landed in Plymouth Bay, had forced Americans to develop certain skills and habits of the heart. It had taught them self-sufficiency and it affected everyone equally. The craftsman, the farmer, the surgeon, the politician: on the frontier all Americans had to carve their places in the world out of the wilderness.

The *Last of the Mohicans* is a novel by James Fenimore Cooper, published in 1826, just five years before de Tocqueville made his observations of America. The story takes place seventy years earlier during the French-Indian War, but it captures the same American frontier character that de Tocqueville met. The 1992 movie version has this great exchange between a British military officer and an aristocratic young woman from England who longs to join the Americans in their frontier lifestyle:

Major Heyward: And who empowered these colonials to pass judgement on England's policies, and to come and go without so much as a "by your leave?"

Cora Munro: They do not live their lives "by your leave!" They hack it out of the wilderness with their own two hands, bearing their children along the way!

This was the essence of the American character from the seventeenth century until sometime around the turn of the twentieth. The ever-expanding frontier gave most of us the opportunity to go most anywhere and try most anything. It certainly didn't guarantee success, but more than in any nation on Earth up to that point, it gave most Americans the freedom to invent their own lives and identities. Europeans, carried along by social inertia that started before Caesar's legions conquered Gaul, didn't necessarily expect those things from life. In 1893, at the Chicago World's Fair, historian Frederick Jackson Turner expanded on de Tocqueville's observations. His famous "Frontier Thesis" argued that during the process of settling the North American continent, generations of European (and we might add

Asian) immigrants began to perceive the relationship between society and individual freedom differently. They became Americans.

So who were these pioneers, living in log cabins? Crude, rude, uneducated bumpkins? Hillbillies without a knowledgeable perspective on the larger world? Listen to de Tocqueville, a French nobleman whose family fought at the Battle of Hastings in 1066, describe the Americans he met living in log cabins on the frontier in 1831:

> *The traveler who approaches one of them [log cabins] towards nightfall sees the flicker of the hearth flame through the chinks in the walls; and at night, if the wind rises, he hears the roof of boughs shake to and fro in the midst of the great forest trees. Who would not suppose that this poor hut is the asylum of rudeness and ignorance? Yet no sort of comparison can be drawn between the pioneer and the dwelling that shelters him. Everything about him is primitive and wild, but he is himself the result of the labor and experience of eighteen centuries. He wears the dress and speaks the language of cities; he is acquainted with the past, curious about the future, and ready for argument about the present; he is, in short, a highly civilized being, who consents for a time to inhabit the backwoods, and who penetrates into the wilds of the New World with the Bible, an axe, and some newspapers. It is difficult to imagine the incredible rapidity with which thought circulates in the midst of these deserts [the wilderness].* ***I do not think that so much intellectual activity exists in the most enlightened and populous districts of France.*** *[emphasis added].*

That is an apt description of the ideals that shaped America: freedom, self-determination, education, risk taking, self-employment. Of course not every American lived that way, and even those who did didn't always live up to those ideals. If it's fair to talk about a nation's hopes, dreams and character, those are America's. They were not Europe's, or China's or India's.

Americans sometimes can't see the forest for the trees: we don't understand how unique our national experience has been. We assume that everyone values personal liberty, the ability to invent your own identity, the right to be your own boss. Those things come so naturally to us and feel so right that we can't imagine anyone else not feeling the same way. So we ascribe their hesitation to accept American values as cowardice or weakness or stupidity. We had that kind of limited perspective already in 1831, when de Tocqueville noticed that:

> *I have lived much with the people in the United States, and cannot express how much I admire their experience and their good sense. An American should never be led to speak of Europe, for he will then probably display much presumption and very foolish pride. He will take up with those crude and vague notions which are so useful to the ignorant all over the world.*

However, he went on, we did know what our freedom was because we participated in the process of continuing to "invent" America.

> *But if you question him respecting his own country, the cloud that dimmed his intelligence will immediately disperse; his language will become as clear and precise as his thoughts. He will inform you what his rights are and by what means he exercises them; he will be able to*

> *point out the customs which obtain in the political world. You will find that he is well acquainted with the rules of the administration, and that he is familiar with the mechanism of the laws. The citizen of the United States does not acquire his practical science and his positive notions from books; the instruction he has acquired may have prepared him for receiving those ideas, but it did not furnish them. The American learns to know the laws by participating in the act of legislation; and he takes a lesson in the forms of government from governing. The great work of society is ever going on before his eyes and, as it were, under his hands.*

OK, you say, that was then, but this is now. Hasn't the frontier been gone for over a hundred years? Are those still our ideals in the twenty-first century? Should they be?

Actually, America still has a literal frontier. When Frederick Jackson Turner presented his famous thesis at the Chicago World's Fair in 1893 he argued that the frontier was "closed," because the population density of the Great Plains had risen above 6 people per square mile. Ironically, it is fallen back below that now. Over the last thirty years or so the Plains are depopulating as economic and demographic shifts drive young people to the cities. There are now large tracts of plains states with densities below 2 persons per square mile. The 2000 Census showed that Kansas has more "frontier" counties now than it did in 1900, and 35 of the 53 counties in North Dakota qualify as "frontier." Any American that wants to can still try to carve an existence from the prairie. Land is cheap out there, especially these days. As to what you would do for a living...well, that's the beauty of it: you're free to demonstrate American ingenuity and self-determination through hard work.

In another sense, the frontier shifted in the twentieth century from geography to economics and technology. As the open spaces were settled, Americans used their freedom and self-determination to build the most prosperous, dynamic and technologically-advanced society the world had ever known. GI's who came back from World War II may have lived in little stucco houses instead of log cabins, but like their great, great grandfathers, they believed that they were free to go anywhere and try anything that they could imagine. African-Americans, exceptions to the principles of freedom and self-determination, began to claim those ideals for themselves in the Civil Rights Movement during the 1960s, a century after the Civil War.

Of course not all Americans have always been free: African Americans, Native Americans, Mexican Americans, women, etc. Personal liberty and self-determination haven't been universally enjoyed throughout American history. Still, the ideal of freedom is not invalidated because it wasn't perfectly implemented. The very concept of personal liberty would never have been developed if we hadn't aspired to and reached toward it as a nation. As a people, we value it enough to have, gradually and sometimes grudgingly, made it universal. America's heritage, and our gift to the world, has been the idea of personal liberty and self-determination. It has not been perfect, perfectly executed, or perfectly received, but without America's long, difficult effort to realize its own ideals the world would not have known it as much as it has.

America has changed in recent decades. We've become more urban, more domesticated, more technological, more connected through large institutions...and maybe more controlled by the larger society around us. Our "national conversation" has shifted. We talk less about individual freedom and more about social responsibility. Maybe that's a good thing...how can we be *against* social responsibility? Of course we must recognize that we live in communities and our actions affect our neighbors in many ways. We've always understood that our individual rights must in some ways be limited by their potential affect others. In 1919, in the case of *Schenck vs. United States,* the Supreme Court famously said that the right to free speech does not give someone a right to falsely shout, "Fire!" in a crowded theater and cause a panic. Americans have never thought freedom to be the right to do anything you want regardless of the consequences for others. The starting point of our national conversation now seems to be the needs of society and what we owe it rather than the rights of the individual to live as he or she sees fit.

That was the starting point for Europeans, born into a place and a position. Your family might have been blacksmiths in a particular village for six generations and society expected you to take your turn. That was your social responsibility. We began this book by talking about the village of Farnham in 1348. As we saw, what was so remarkable about the generation that lived through the Black Death is that their society was shaken up as if you had shaken a box of Legos, spilling half of them in process and then having to rebuild a Lego sculpture with what remained. It gave them, for a few generations at least, more freedom and mobility than they had known for centuries. We're living through the reverse of that: our society is becoming more controlling, and we have less personal freedom than Americans have ever known before.

Is that bad? Maybe we *should* be less free. Maybe we need to accept that the twenty-first century is an urbanized, networked, global culture. Americans are not and cannot be cowboys anymore. We need to ask whether all of our individual wants and needs are really good for our community. We need to consider whether the frontier mentality is ecologically, economically and politically sustainable.

If we surrender the American character of personal liberty, who do we surrender it to? What replaces it? If we don't make our own choices, who does make them? On what basis? The "community?" What's "the community?" Who speaks for it? Who makes the rules in its name? The culture or society at large? Same questions. The government? Well, which government: local, state, or federal? Which branch? Which politicians or judges or bureaucrats? Under what terms? How much power should they have to limit our freedoms? Should Harvard grads in Washington tell Montanans how fast they can drive down their highways? Should lobbyists and midlevel regulators on the East Coast tell local micro-brewers in Texas how to bottle their beer? What about schools? Who should decide how my kid is educated? The federal government? Why? To protect my kid from my bad parenting choices? Where does the government's authority over my child overrule mine? Who's kid is it, anyway?

What about our sweet, sweet vices? What about smoking or unsafe sex or not wearing seat belts or eating transfats or emitting CO2 or base jumping? As a society we are increasingly limiting those for two reasons: 1) if you do bad things it might have an impact on the rest of us who have to pay for it, and 2) it's our social responsibility to save people from themselves.

For some these choices are easy: they assume that all the official nannies of the Nanny State are altruistic and transparent. If you raise your hand and ask them to explain how the regulators know what's best for all of us, you risk being called an "antigovernment wingnut."

We are right to ask who will make those decisions for us. Do "They" (whoever "They" are) think that individuals--we common, average Americans--are too stupid or too lazy or ignorant or depraved to make our own choices? We very well may be stupid, lazy, ignorant and depraved...but who, exactly, is going to be our nanny? Who is going to watch over us?

And there's this: who will watch the watchers? Socrates asked that question in Plato's *Republic:* if we put guardians in charge of the State to protect us from ourselves and each other, who will guard the guardians? More pointedly: who will protect us from our protectors? Plato's answer was disappointing. He said that we would tell the guardians a "noble lie:" that they are smarter and better than the ordinary citizens and that it is their moral responsibility to guard and protect those who are less wise and capable. They would be like parents--or nannies--protecting children from doing foolish things.

See, maybe it's just me, but I'm not totally cool with that. I love the idea of social responsibility and the government preventing stupid people from doing stupid things. I can't wrap my brain around the "noble lie" because I suspect that the noble lie today involves an Ivy League degree, connections in Washington D.C. and supposed expertise in a variety of subjects. I don't trust the wisdom of those things as much as "They" would like me to.

As I said, my life is a cautionary tale about the risks of freedom, self-determination and self-employment. Albertus Van Raalte and the founders of my town, 10 years after *Democracy in America* was published, were exactly the kind of pioneers that Alexis de Tocqueville and Frederick Jackson Turner described. They left the Netherlands with its rules and rigid social categories. They nearly froze to death trying to get to West Michigan. When they arrived they found nothing but deep woods and swamps. They really did carve clearings from the forest and build log cabin homes and churches. They dredged the swamps and dug a channel to connect their community to Lake Michigan. They built a town and a liberal arts college to teach Greek and Latin in the wilderness. Over time that experience shaped them, and they became Americans.

I inherited their sense of freedom, adventure and self-determination. I wasn't disciplined by their experience. I sold and wheeled and dealed. I "built" a custom executive home in the forest as well, but only in the sense that I told the real builder what I wanted and signed loan papers. I bought even more houses on credit, some of them virtually on top of the sites where the pioneer settlers had cleared the land and built their cabins 150 years earlier. They did it to build a community, I did it to flip them quickly for profit. It didn't work out like I thought it would.

In the end I valued freedom, but didn't have the experience or maturity to manage it. What should have been done? Should I have been forced to stay in school? Should a government official have had to review and approve my career? Who was supposed to watch over me, to guard me from my own foolish exuberance? If there had been someone like that, who should have been watching him to protect the rest of us?

Chapter 11
"Go Outside"

Here's another clipping for the "Only in America" file: during the Great Recession we're getting fatter.

According to a food industry group that does annual surveys on eating patterns and health, and quoted in the Wall Street Journal in October 2009, our butts are getting bigger even as our bank accounts are getting smaller. How is this possible? Aren't the poor lean and hungry? Don't rich people spend the day sitting around eating little cakes while skinny immigrants carry their golf clubs and wash their Bentleys?

Apparently not. In yet another way Generation X has changed the world, now the rich are skinny and carry their own clubs while the poor sit around eating little cakes: Twinkies, Ding Dong's, McDonald's Hot Apple Pies and Little Debbie Strawberry Shortcake Rolls. How can this be?

First, junk food is cheap. Fresh meats and vegetables and other non-processed whole foods are expensive. Generally, you can't buy the components for a healthy meal, a fresh salad and roast chicken for example, for what it costs to order a meal off the dollar menu at any fast-food joint. Even at the grocery store, much less mini-marts, the less expensive packaged food is high in calories and fat with little nutritional value. Why? Is this some corporate conspiracy to create a lumpy underclass? No, it's just simple economics. It costs more to create, transport and retail high-quality and rapidly perishable vegetables and meats. Especially now that we bring produce from all around the world so that we can get any type of fruit in any growing season in any grocery store. Want a crunchy apple in January? No problem, check the produce aisle: they were flown in yesterday from Argentina. The same thing is true with the salmon or a hundred other products. On the other hand, a bag of potato chips, a frozen pot pie or a box of macaroni and cheese is an industrial product that is made, transported, stored and retailed easily at low price points. The same "economies of scale" occurred to the pizza places when they figured out that by making a steady stream of "hot and ready" pizzas they could drop the price to five or six dollars. It's hard to mix a nice salad and grill some halibut for that. The rich can afford not to eat fast food. During the recession more of us are grazing on junk food all the time.

That's not the only reason that the rich are skinny, the middle class are lumpy and the poor are fat. How does one explain the other factors in a politically and culturally sensitive way? The higher one moves on the economic and social ladder the more value is placed on appearance and physical fitness. Have you walked around a WalMart lately? I appreciate WalMart as a retailer, but many of their customers do not appear to be compulsive about exercise, fashion or even grooming. I have no data, but I'm willing to bet dollars to donuts (pun intended) that there is a correlation in America today between income and activity levels and self-discipline. Based on my casual observation, it appears to me that, not only are wealthier people more likely to belong to and use a gym, they're more likely to jog, walk the dog and have active hobbies like hiking or bike riding. Some of that is because they have more financial resources, of course, but not entirely. Most Americans could, if they really wanted to, walk their dog or go for a day hike in a state park. Instead, it seems that the lower one moves on the socioeconomic ladder the more sedentary the lifestyle becomes. I guess that not too many rich people spend much time watching television while they eat snacks and update their Facebook.

I'm no sociologist, so I don't know what the cause and effect relationship is here. Are active, fit and self-disciplined people more likely to climb the economic ladder, so that they do better in school, achieve more in business, and marry other good looking and active people? Or is it the other way around: because they are part of the higher classes are they more likely to engage in "culturally correct" activities? Surely anyone who went to high school, worked in sales or watched a political campaign has noticed that good-looking, well-dressed, energetic, self-disciplined and outgoing people are more popular. They attract each other and are more likely to make a sale or get hired. Since life seems to reward their behaviors, maybe that just reinforces their inclination to eat well, stay fit and dress stylishly. Maybe the rest of us just give up sometime after high school when we realize that we aren't going to rise to the top of the heap. Maybe we just give up and become lumpy and lazy, spending our evenings watching *American Idol* while we eat giant plates of cheese nachos.

Sometimes you find an example that so perfectly captures the essence of a situation that it goes beyond being merely symbolic and becomes *iconic.* The iconic parable for the problem I'm describing in this chapter is Chinese "gold farming" companies. Some of you know what I'm talking about, and if you do then you may be part of the problem.

There is a computer game called *World of Warcraft.* It's an online, medieval-like universe where players (in this world) pay a monthly fee to create a character and "live" through it a "life" of adventure with quests and battles in the virtual world. But adventure isn't cheap. While the monthly fee (this world) is only a few dollars, the armor, weapons and other cool stuff inside the *World of Warcraft* cost gold coins. Lots of them. So the players (in this world) have their characters (in there) perform relatively simple tasks, like hunting boars in the virtual woods or digging in gold mines, to earn (imaginary) gold coins. Are you with me?

The problem is that all these gold-coin-earning activities are time consuming (here) and even *World of Warcraft* players sometimes have to perform real-world tasks like eating, bathing and holding down a job (some of them). And while they're performing real-world chores and earning real-world money they can't be doing imaginary chores and earning imaginary money. Talk about an opportunity-cost dilemma! Have no fear, though, for we have created the most awesome, global, wired marketplace the world has ever known. What's more, in that marketplace Generation X can always rely on the Chinese to bail us out of our financial predicaments: enter Chinese gold farming.

Take a minute and enter that into your search engine: Chinese gold farming. You'll find Wikipedia entries, articles and lots of advertisements for gold-farming companies. I found a great article from March 2009 on the UK *Guardian's* website. What you'll discover is that Chinese companies, always ready to meet any economic demand, have offices crammed full of computer terminals. They hire basically unskilled young men to sit at these terminals and play *World of Warcraft* for their clients. Americans can go to these companies' websites and order services: they want their character to earn so much gold, to level up by performing tasks or to find some magic weapon in the game. The customer enters his credit card number and goes to sleep (probably), work (maybe) or on a date (doubtful). Meanwhile, at a terminal set up on a folding table in a nondescript office building in China some young man on a ten-hour shift receives the electronic work-order. He logs into the customer's game account and plays his character for him: looting a village, hunting for pelts or fighting some mythological beast. The gold farmers interviewed said they don't really enjoy the game, it's a factory job like so many others in China. When their shift is over they get a bowl of rice with vegetables and meat and sleep in the next room on bunk beds until it's time to "go into the mines" again. It's a job.

When the American customer wakes up or gets home he (I'm operating on the assumption that the vast majority of these customers are male) eagerly logs into his *World of Warcraft* account to happily discover that he is "richer" and "more powerful" than he was the last time he checked (except that in the real world his credit card balance is $20 higher).

This book is about Generation X, the *Star Wars* generation, growing up. This makes me question whether that's even possible. We have to own this one, guys: it's probably not teenagers or baby boomers, and certainly not the World War II generation, that are running up credit card balances by outsourcing their fantasy role play to Chinese sweatshops. This may be the saddest commentary on our generation yet: we're now, officially, too lazy to play our own video games.

Whatever the reasons, the bottom line on our bottoms is that we keep getting less healthy. Which is ironic, since we are wrapped up in a national brouhaha about how to provide better and cheaper health care. As I listen to experts debate the ins and outs of medical insurance, public options and cost containment, I realize that I have no idea how to fix the healthcare industry. Still, I do have a modest proposal for our generation, which I think just might contribute to the success of whatever system we adopt.

Let's all go outside and play.

Seriously, that's the best I've got. Not brilliant or original, but I feel pretty good about it. It's like the navy blazer of healthcare solutions: traditional, dependable, always in style.

What if we changed our lifestyles? What if we spent more time walking the dog, riding a bike when we need to go places, going to the park and throwing a Frisbee? Instead of watching TV or playing *World of Warcraft*, what if we shot baskets on the driveway or at a local park or school? Some of us like to walk around the mall, but that can be depressing if you have no cash and counterproductive if you're munching a cinnamon roll the size of a dinner plate while you do it. What if we spent a Saturday afternoon going on a day hike at a county or state park instead? When we're driving somewhere, like on an overnight trip, what if--just hear me out, because I know this is a crazy idea--we didn't always stop for fast food? What if we pulled off at one of those rest areas along the side of the highway and ate a sandwich that we had packed from home and then walked around a little bit? I can think of a thousand examples that don't involve much money or strenuous exercise but would get us outdoors and active. That's how previous generations lived. Take a look at clothing sizes from forty or fifty years ago. If you can find an old suit or dress or army uniform your grandparents wore when they were you're age, I'm willing to bet that most of us couldn't fit into it. Not everyone was a laborer or athlete but they were thinner and healthier than we are because they ate less and exercised more. Just that simple.

Let's be realistic, having more active, outdoor lifestyles won't defeat cancer, thwart viruses, prevent genetic disorders or bring down the cost of MRI machines. Getting off our enormous butts and spending more time outdoors isn't a cure-all, but I can think of at least seven benefits to that sort of lifestyle.

1. ***If we were more fit and active we would be generally healthier and reduce some of our medical costs.*** The fact that other countries, like France or Switzerland, have less heart surgeons,

is often used as indictment of their socialized healthcare systems. That may be true, but it also may be true (as I have seen reports, but I'm not an expert) that the French have less incidence of heart disease because they eat less and thus weigh less and are generally more active. Insurers and employers who pay for insurance have, for some time, given discounts for people who can show that they lose weight, exercise more and avoid unhealthy behaviors like smoking and excessive drinking. Is this the nanny state or just market economics? Healthier people cost insurers less. As I said, it won't help you avoid injury in a car crash, a genetic disorder, some types of cancer or a viral epidemic. It will probably lower your risk for heart disease, diabetes and some forms of cancer (which are all big-ticket items in the health insurance business). If you do get sick or injured, it probably increases your resilience and ability to respond to treatment. If we all spent more time playing and working outside, our health and healthcare system would both benefit.

2. ***Not only would we be healthier, we'd be happier as well.*** I have no data to back this up, other than common sense. If we spent more time playing with the kids at the park, walking the dog or taking a Sunday afternoon hike with a picnic lunch, and less time watching TV, surfing the web, or buying stuff, we'd be less stressed and emotionally healthier. I'm not saying it will solve all our problems, but fresh air and exercise are incredible antidotes for our affluenza. It's also a powerful defense against manipulation by the Society of the Spectacle.

If everyone playing Farmville on Facebook or wandering through virtual woods in the *World of Warcraft* visited a real farm or forest from time to time they might find life to be richer and more fulfilling.

3. ***We would be a "greener" society.*** Using our cars less and our legs more would reduce our carbon output and stress our environment less. I'm not suggesting that we can all commute to work on a bike, but even small changes in our lifestyle add up. We would improve our environment and become more sensitive to it if we spend more time outdoors.

4. ***This might be a little airy-fairy, but I think that our spiritual health would improve as well.*** There's no magic to being outdoors, of course, and homeless people or people in primitive cultures aren't spiritually superior just because they spend more hours outside. I do believe that spending time in God's creation can make us more appreciative of the Creator. Our souls can only be improved by spending less time plugged into the noise and consumerism of electronic media. Thirty minutes walking without those distractions is thirty minutes of reflection and greater awareness of nature and our neighborhood. That can't help but develop us as people.

5. ***We might get along better if we spent more time outdoors together.*** What happens when a husband and wife come home

from work and eat a pizza in front of a TV while surfing the web? Well, they might enjoy that as a pleasant evening, but I'm convinced that if they more often took a walk together or did yard work together or joined a church softball league together, their relationship would improve. We interact with each other differently when we are outdoors, doing something with someone. We can pay attention to them in ways we don't when we're being passively entertained or consuming. We bond together in the sight, smell and touch of nature and each other. It's also a no-brainer, I think, that parents should spend time outside playing with their kids. Yes, you can stick them in front of a game console or take them to a movie. Nothing, however, bonds and makes memories like flying a kite or hitting a ball or going on a long hike until your legs are aching and you plop down in a picnic area to eat the sandwiches you brought. Those are moments that change lives.

6. ***Our self-image and our world-image might improve.*** Many people in other countries perceive Americans to be fat and lazy. The truth is that many of us see ourselves that way. We didn't build this country and create its infrastructure and wealth. Our grandparents' generation did that, and they did it by being more energetic and active than we are. If we spent more time outdoors and exercising, we might begin to see ourselves as an energetic and healthy society, and others might as well.

7. **A final, cheerful thought:** if we spent more time outdoors, getting stronger, more energetic and healthier, maybe our kids won't grow up to be tubby little consumers, paying Chinese kids to play their video games for them. In fact, they might be strong enough to defend us when the Chinese hordes arrive to collect all the real-world money we borrowed from them to fund our consumer lifestyles.

Chapter 12
"Land of the Best and Least Governed"

There's a scene in the hilarious 1999 movie *Office Space* in which the main character, played by Ron Livingston, is arguing with his girlfriend, played by Jennifer Anniston. She's a waitress at a restaurant that makes the staff wear suspenders decorated with random little joke buttons they call "pieces of flair." He's frustrated with her and losing the argument. Not knowing what else to say, he blurts out, "You know the Nazis had pieces of flair, that they made the Jews wear!" "What?!" she exclaims, with a look of disbelief.

It's a perfect example of Godwin's Law and *reductio ad Hitlerum.* You may have never heard of Godwin's Law, but I'll bet you've seen it in action plenty of times. Michael Godwin is an attorney and author, who practices mostly in the field of Internet law. In 1990 he proposed the following Law: "As a Usenet discussion [Internet discussion or comment thread] grows longer, the probability of a comparison involving Nazis or Hitler approaches 1 [or 100%]." In other words, once we start arguing about something on the Internet it is inevitable that someone gets called a Nazi. You can bet the family farm on it.

The term *Reductio ad Hitlerum* was first coined by University of Chicago professor Leo Strauss in 1953. It's a ridiculous type of logical fallacy that asserts that since Hitler or the Nazis did something, anyone else who does the same thing must therefore be a new Hitler or a Nazi. Thus in *Office Space* the Ron Livingston character, having no better comeback to Jennifer Anniston, resorts to pointing out that the Nazis made people wear little emblems, and since she works for a company that makes its employees wear little pieces of flair...well, the implication is *obvious:* she's a Nazi (!).

Godwin's Law has made the jump from Internet discussion threads to everyday politics. Pick any controversial topic: taxes, healthcare, war, school funding, gay marriage or funding for PBS. Once the protestors, pundits and politicians get to even a mild boil there's going to be a Hitler analogy and someone's going to get called a Nazi. Set your watch by it.

While the reductio ad Hitlerum is easily the most popular name-calling tactic, it's not the only one. In recent years the *reductio ad Marxum,* calling someone a Marxist, has run a respectable second place. Old favorites like the *reductio ad Klanum* (comparing someone to the Ku Klux Klan) is an old favorite as is the *reductio ad McCarthum* (comparing them to Senator Joseph McCarthy) and the *reductio ad Torquemadum* (comparing someone to Thomas de Torquemada, the head of the Spanish Inquisition that tried heretics during the Renaissance).

These are silly arguments for a lot of reasons, not the least of which is that they're simply lazy. Instead of making the effort to criticize an opponent accurately it's just stupid name calling. Don't get me wrong: there are people, programs and ideologies that should be fought against. Sometimes the issues are so important that these ridiculous *reductio* arguments aren't strong and serious *enough.* No one takes them seriously anymore. Calling someone a Nazi or a Marxist doesn't necessarily score any points, but a more accurate argument might make a real difference in a debate.

Furthermore, it cheapens the term: some ideas *are* Marxist, or Nazi-like, or racist, or whatever. I would rather we save our ammo: when we call someone a Nazi or a Marxist, I want it to mean something.

America has some very real and difficult problems that require clear thinking and bold action. In America circa 2010 almost all public debates devolve into shouting matches and name calling. How can we get anything done if we can't even talk to each other? Unless we can communicate constructively we can't cooperate productively.

Why can't we have intelligent arguments about public policy in America anymore? As I said above, some of it is laziness: it's easier to lump everyone into big categories (Nazis, Marxists, etc.) than to engage them accurately (even when an accurate criticism might be more devastating). Another reason is that our technology gives no time for self-editing. We've been talking throughout this book about the consequences of us having such powerful communications technologies at our fingertips. Sometimes this allows us to publicly broadcast things we haven't thought about enough. In the past, if you wanted to publish your thoughts the time and steps in that process might have made you reconsider your words. Now we can blurt out any dumb thought that pops into our head on Facebook in real time.

I don't think that either of those are the real reason why we shout at each other and toss "Hitler" around in our public debates. I think that it's because we never talk about the *real* differences between us. The issues on the table are usually symptoms or reflections of our deeper political philosophies and worldviews. When any of us support policies for immigration, war, healthcare, education, taxation or marriage rights, we are usually supporting a method of enacting our values. Our policies are means to ends. As long as we are working toward *different* ends we will never agree about the policies. So we talk past each other, shout and throw names around. Shouldn't we discuss the real differences between us? Wouldn't it be more productive to debate about our values and worldviews? At least it would be honest.

Some people are, in fact, Marxists. They understand the world through Marxist categories and have Marxist values. When arguing about almost any public policy that worldview is relevant and drives any practical solutions they propose. They should be honest enough to admit it, and the debate will be more productive if that's understood by everyone involved. Equally, some people are fascists, nihilists, racists, capitalists or Islamists. Some of us aspire to live in a democratic republic while others really would be more comfortable in an opportunistic kleptocracy. Some of us really believe in a Madisonian flavor of American exceptionalism while some of us, honestly, do hate the legacy of Western civilization and the traditions of the United States.

Reread that last paragraph. You might find it boring or confusing. Maybe you don't know what all those words mean. It's OK if you don't, but they are the keys to understanding why America is politically stalemated. Those big ideas, those worldviews, are the real differences between us. If you want to understand the issues that divide us and be a useful contributor to the debates that will shape America for the next fifty years, then you can begin by learning what those terms, and others, mean. If not, you can always just keep calling Bush a Nazi or Obama a Marxist.

Talking about worldviews and political philosophies is hard. They are complicated topics, rooted in abstract values. They wrestle with questions like: *What is the goal of society? How should the interests of the individual be weighed against the interests of the community? Where does the power of the government come from? What, if anything, are the members of society entitled to from that society? How should those things be guaranteed or delivered?* People have been arguing about these things ever since humans began living in groups. Serious philosophers began writing about these around three thousand years ago in Israel, China, Egypt, India and Greece. The Greek philosopher Plato laid the groundwork for how Western civilization would approach these questions in *The Republic* and his other writings during the fifth century B.C.

Some of you are already bored. Almost everyone I know thinks that philosophy is boring, but I don't know anyone who isn't highly opinionated about these questions. That tells me that the issues aren't boring, but perhaps the way that they are taught or written about often is. Academia isn't much help because most academic philosophy has often become esoteric, and bears no relationship to how these questions are hashed out in real life. Conservative intellectuals left academia a generation ago because they couldn't get tenure and fled to think tanks and foundations. Liberals especially love to imagine how great society would be if only the government could be led by an all-star team of Ivy League professors. In their ideal Camelot, we would be governed by "czars:" experts expertly exercising their expertise. Some left-wing readers may want to close their eyes for a moment, imagining what a happy, well-run nation we would be. Personally, I agree with conservative William F. Buckley, Jr., who once said that he'd rather live in a society governed by the first four hundred names in the Boston phone book than by the faculty of Harvard University.

Still, there are plenty of hard and boring subjects that have huge effects on our daily lives: tax law, bridge design, pharmaceutical chemistry. If we do not figure these things out for ourselves someone else will do it for us. Politicians, judges, lobbyists, activists, special interests all know what they are trying to accomplish, as well as why and how to do it. People who can talk about these worldview issues clearly and compellingly are rare. Even rarer are people who cannot only talk about them, but lead and organize other people in doing something about them. We toss Karl Marx's name around because he changed history by articulating a worldview in such a unique way that it changed history. We need to understand the views of people like

Adam Smith, Karl Marx, Mao Zedong, Winston Churchill and Ronald Reagan. If we leave the big picture questions to others we'll be left to arguing about the details and calling anyone we disagree with "Hitler!"

Americans usually consider talking about these big-picture worldviews as rude and unfair. There are good reasons for that rooted in America's founding traditions and model of government. The Constitution of the United States is a work of genius that allows people who disagree about abstract issues still cooperate in practical matters. It is brilliantly silent about some big questions (what is the "general welfare" that it is supposed to be promoted?), and simply precise about procedural mechanisms. The Founding Fathers were intellectuals, products of the Enlightenment who knew better than anyone that differences in values and worldviews could paralyze a nation. They invented a country in which people could argue about *where?* and *why?* but could nevertheless work together on the *what do we do now?* This is the art of political compromise. The nineteenth century German politician Otto Van Bismark once called politics "the art of the possible" because the trick is to discover not what everyone ideally wants, but what we can actually get done. Our Constitution and political traditions are practical instruments, and have been cleverly engineered to avoid public debates about worldviews and philosophies.

For example, we all like to complain about our two-party system. What's the alternative? Most other industrialized countries have a parliamentary system with lots of parties. France and the United

Kingdom both have dozens of political parties and Germany seems lean by comparison with only six parties that currently hold seats in their parliament. A parliamentary system allows you to form a political party around any ideology that you want, no matter how narrow. In France, for example, the "Hunting, Fishing, Nature and Tradition" party (obviously) represents the worldview of people who want to preserve traditional rural values of hunting and fishing in nature. In the last elections it got less than 2% of the first-round votes in parliamentary elections. The French Communist Party, people who really *are* Marxists, got less than 4%. In parliamentary systems like this, people vote for representatives that narrowly represent their values. After that, coalitions are formed in the parliament around practical issues, and the parliament then appoints the executive branch (the prime minister and his cabinet) based on the deals made in those coalitions. The compromising is done by the politicians *after* the election.

In contrast, the American system forces coalitions to be formed in our *primary* elections. Within the Democratic and Republican parties alliances of convenience are made between voters with wildly different interests and philosophies. The Democrats' primaries cobble together people who don't have the same worldview at all: socialists, blue collar union workers, academics, pro-life Hispanics, pacifists, military families, gay-rights activists, and both traditional blacks and traditional segregationists. Republican primaries do the same, forcing sometimes uneasy alliances between evangelical Christians, libertarians, pro-military types, free market capitalists and both isolationists and those who favor a pro-active involvement in world affairs. All of these arguments occur within the parties before the general election, and when a new congress or president is inaugurated their mandate is usually formed around some list of practical policies. The difference between our two-party and the rest of the world's multi-party systems is where the political coalitions are built. In America, they are built, to a large degree, by the voters before the politicians get seated in the legislature. That is part of the genius of our system.

The tension between the states and the federal government has existed in our political system since the Declaration of independence was signed. After the Revolutionary War, we lived under something called the Articles of Confederation for eleven years. Each state was essentially an independent country, issuing its own currency. There was no federal government, no national military or courts. It didn't work, so in 1787 representatives of the states met to write a constitution. In that Constitutional Convention the arguments largely revolved around the balance of power between the federal government and the states. How, the Founding Fathers wondered, could we be one nation with an effective federal government, and yet remain a group of united *states?* James Madison recorded the debates in *The Federalist Papers,* and it is remarkable how the issues have remained to this day. Should the federal government be able to regulate healthcare, restrict gun ownership or dictate school curriculum? Should those powers be left to states or even individual communities?

Slavery was already tearing this country apart during the Constitutional Convention. Many provisions in the Constitution and later political compromises were an attempt to hold the nation together. The Civil War resulted from the power struggle between federal and state powers. Abraham Lincoln agonized over this inherent conflict. In the Gettysburg Address he said, *"Now we are engaged in a great civil war, testing whether that nation, or any nation, so conceived and so dedicated, can long endure."* In the speech he was talking about "the proposition that all men are created equal," but the larger context was, and still is, whether a nation of people with wildly different worldviews can long endure. Will such a nation inevitably fracture, or will it be forced to limit rights and suppress some values in order to preserve unity?

So, what are we supposed to do?

First, I have to say that we need to be committed to pluralism and diversity. We always have to say that. Political Correctness demands that our first and greatest commandment is "commitment to diversity." O.K.?

Second, we need to be committed to the United States Constitution. While there is no serious danger to diversity of thought, speech, or interest groups in America today, our Constitution is under constant assault. Truthfully, it's been under constant assault since the document was completed on September 17, 1787. It is a document made to be tested. Our values and worldviews grind hard against each other and for over two hundred years the Constitution has been the only grease that keeps them turning. In our lifetime that friction has only gotten worse. As in the decades leading up to the Civil War, we are deeply divided about our vision of America and its identity. We no longer have the language to speak to each other, and are dangerously close to being unable to work together in any practical way. The old issues, the ones that James Madison recorded in The Federalist Papers are still with us: the balance of power between federal and state government, the rights of the individual versus government mandates, the government's power to tax us and create public debt, etc. Throughout American history we have had periods of greater and lesser agreement on these questions, but our generation inherits a time of such deep division and animosity that consensus is a fantasy. Everyone, on all sides, finds the Constitution an inconvenience to their agenda, but we are quick to point out how the views held by our opposition are unconstitutional. We look for favorable executive orders, favorable court rulings, or outright legislative power to enforce our values. If we allow the Constitution to be chipped away in pursuit of anyone's political ideals, we face the very real prospect of fracturing as a nation. If one side enacts what the other side considers to be Marxism or the other side considers to be fascism, we won't just be hurling insults. Don't think it can't happen in our lifetime.

Third, we have to be willing, and able, to talk intelligently about our values, philosophies and worldviews. We can argue about healthcare policy for another fifty years, but the reason we can't agree isn't that we haven't hit just the right policy formulation. The healthcare debate divides us for the same reasons that slavery, segregation or abortion have divided us: our worldviews are so far apart. As I write this, the federal government is in the midst of legislating a reinvention of the healthcare industry in the U.S. The debate won't be over for years, as legislators and lawyers argue about whether the bill is even constitutional. This process will polarize our nation even further. Not only does the policy tread into unchartered constitutional waters, it taps into our deepest beliefs about the rights of man, the tension between the individual and the community, the nature of the state, and our idea of the greatest good. These are the very issues that the characters in Plato's *Republic* sat around and debated 2,500 years ago, and they couldn't agree. Barack Obama likes to say, "The time for bickering is over." Really? What he means is that in his mind the big-picture questions are settled and all that's left is the details of implementing his vision. Conservatives have been guilty of similar statements. In reality, we need to recognize that the debate about policy only shows that the time for bickering *isn't* over. We shouldn't be afraid to say to each other that we don't just reject their policy, we reject the premises on which it is based. Then we need to be able to do that without name calling.

Of course, we shouldn't be afraid to label something for what it is. If someone really does believe in socialism, fascism or whatever else, shouldn't they be willing to fly their flag and admit it? What's wrong with calling something what it is, as long as the label is accurate?

In his 1849 essay *Civil Disobedience,* Henry David Thoreau said that, "That government is best which governs least." Some say that he got that from either Thomas Paine or Thomas Jefferson. Truthfully, it was a popular idea among the Founding Fathers. As Generation X takes its turn leading America, we need to remember that after we finish arguing about our values and worldviews (which we must), we have to move on to the Constitutional business of governing. Everything can't become a *reductio ad Hitlerum, ad absurdum* (until it's absurd), *ad nauseatum* (until we puke).

That means that the United States will have a minimalist government, *by design.* Unable to agree on giant, sweeping visions of the world, we will (hopefully) leave each other alone and focus on practical compromises that create a government that is best when it governs least.

Chapter 13
"Question Everything"

In 1949 George Orwell wrote *1984.* It imagined a future Great Britain (in 1984), which had become a repressive dictatorship. The Party controlled the people by manipulating every aspect of their lives and controlling the flow of information. The single source of public information (news, history, opinion, the sciences, etc.) was the government's "Ministry of Truth" which owned all the media. Newspapers, books, radio, film, television: all were mere agencies of and mouthpieces for the Party. There was no knowledge, only propaganda, and no marketplace for ideas. The world of *1984* was ignorant, stagnant and frightening.

Orwell's premise was that technology would make it easier for the government to control and manipulate information. Along with flying cars and formfitting jumpsuits it was a common vision of the future during the middle of the twentieth century. The assumption wasn't unreasonable as communications technology was expensive. Film studios, radio networks and publishing companies were expensive operations. Only large corporations or governments could afford them, and it seemed likely that as technology developed it would only become more expensive. Futurists had as hard a time imagining individuals broadcasting or publishing information as they did people having their own private navies.

They were wrong. Communications technology is democratizing.

On January 22, 1984, a commercial was broadcast during the Superbowl. That was its first and only commercial airing. Later that year it won the Clio award for best television commercial. In 1995 it was named to the Clio Hall of Fame and *Advertising Age* named it the Greatest Commercial of All Time, as did *TV Guide* in 1999. In 2003 the World Federation of Advertisers gave it their Hall of Fame Golden Jubilee Award and in 2007 it was named the Best Superbowl commercial in the game's forty year history.

The spot is a takeoff of Orwell's *1984.* It opens with Big Brother exhorting rows of dreary and brainwashed worker drones. A young, female athlete is being chased by menacing security police through the corridors of a vast, grey factory. She is carrying a bright sledgehammer and her T-shirt has a sketch of a box that vaguely resembles a television. She runs into an auditorium where workers in drab overalls sit on benches, vacantly staring at a huge screen where Big Brother's face instructs them about "Information Purification Directives" and "Unification of Thoughts." The athlete stops and begins to spin in place, swinging her sledgehammer faster and faster. Just as Big Brother hits his crescendo, boasting, "We shall prevail!" she lets the hammer fly. It smashes into the screen and Big Brother's face explodes, spraying sparks and shards of glass. The commercial ends with the following text: *On January 24th, Apple Computer will introduce Macintosh. And you'll see why 1984 won't be like 1984.* (You can find the video online, just search for "Apple 1984 commercial").

Some of you are rolling your eyes at what you consider to be the typical over-hype of Apple (in the interest of full disclosure this book was written on a Mac and I'm a member of the cult). Even if you're a Microsoft-type, set aside the branding issues and appreciate how prophetic it was. The commercial was proclaiming that personal computers, and the spin-off technologies they led to, would render Orwell's vision impossible.

Throughout this book we've talked about how Generation X has been shaped by growing up during this technology revolution. I've critiqued it and talked about its limitations and negative consequences. Let's be clear about this, though: what we have lived through is something completely new in history. There has never been anything like it. The futurists never saw it coming. It's not just a quantitative, but a *qualitative* leap in the development of civilization. Information and communications technologies have become the mortal foe of dictators, fascists, communists and governments that aspires to central control.

To understand why, we need to talk about an ox-weighing contest that happened at a livestock fair in England in the early nineteenth century. Members of the crowd could walk up, look at an ox, and enter a contest to guess its weight. A scientist and statistician named Sir Francis Galton happened to be there that day, and he noticed something weird. Almost 800 people entered the contest and, of course, no one guessed the correct weight of 1,198 pounds. For whatever reason, Galton got the idea to calculate the average, or the *mean,* of all of their guesses. That was weird (he was a statistician after all), but not the really weird part. This is: the average, or mean, of their guesses was 1,197 pounds, only one pound off the correct weight. Collectively, the crowd was accurate within less than 0.001%.

This story is the opening anecdote in a fantastic book by James Surowiecki, published in 2004, called *The Wisdom of Crowds: Why the Many Are Smarter Than the Few and How Collective Wisdom Shapes Business, Economies, Societies and Nations.* The title is a parody of another influential book from 1841 called *Extraordinary Popular Delusions and the Madness of Crowds* by Scottish journalist Charles Mackay. Mackay warned that if you listened to the crazy notions of the unwashed masses you might end up believing that Bigfoot and the Loch Ness monster were honeymooning in the Bermuda Triangle. Surowiecki argued that crowds can be a lot smarter than that.

Consider the game show Who Wants to be a Millionaire. If you recall, the contestant is asked a series of multiple choice questions for cash prizes that double with each correct answer. The contestant has three "Life Lines" that he or she can use at any point during the game: "50/50," "Phone-a-Friend" and "Ask-the-Audience." Which do you think was the most valuable Life Line, the one that a smart contestant would keep in their pocket until they were really desperate? It wasn't 50/50, since two of the four choices were usually turkeys and the judges would typically take those two away anyway. Phone A Friend sounds good, especially if your friend is an expert in that subject. What if the question is something outside his or her area of expertise? Then they're only guessing, no matter how bright they are. When you used Ask-the-Audience, however, you were getting several hundred independent guesses, from a random cross-section of society. The average of their answers, like the average of the estimates about Galton's ox at the English country fair, had a higher probability of being correct than the guess of any single person. There can be wisdom in a crowd.

Here's another example. The Space Shuttle has five computers that independently calculate its navigation, flight controls and avionics. If any one computer starts rendering numbers that are widely divergent from the others, the rest can "vote" it out of the loop, locking it out of internal system busses. The system has never failed. There can be wisdom in a crowd.

Some of the most accurate predictors of all sorts of events, from who will win on American Idol to who will win the presidency, are online, current-events betting sites like *www.intrade.com*. Thousands, maybe millions, of people are independently gambling real money on outcomes. There can be wisdom in a crowd.

The distributed technologies of the information age make it possible to harness the wisdom of crowds in ways previous generations could never have imagined. Take Wikipedia and other cooperative knowledge bases, for example. It is often pointed out that one cannot trust everything one reads on Wikipedia because anyone can add information to it. That's absolutely correct, and one should always exercise caution when using it. On the other hand, while anyone can add information to it, it's also true that anyone can flag or object to anything posted on Wikipedia. You may add to the Wiki entry about George Washington that he was a cleverly disguised extraterrestrial, with a purple tentacle growing out of his forehead. The pressure of the crowd would come into play, however, and your entry would probably be disputed by thousands of people who don't know each other, all bringing to bear whatever diverse knowledge they have about the first president. More often than not the entry will be corrected quickly.

Consumer product reviews are a great example of harnessing the wisdom of crowds. Professional restaurant, movie and hotel review guides are written by experts with supposedly objective opinions. That's all well and good, but web-based user reviews bring the collective wisdom of the crowd to the surface. Finding out that a new film or a new camera has only two out of five stars based on 2,000 independent user reviews may not do away with the need for professional, expert opinion, but it's pretty important data to consider.

Web-based knowledge projects can collect, collate and distribute information that used to belong only to governments. Google Earth and Google Maps, among others, are vast collaborations between thousands, or millions, of individuals who don't know each other. Everyone contributes some tidbit of information and disputes what they think is incorrect. There are online collaborative information projects about closed countries like North Korea, Cuba or Iran. Anyone who knows something, maybe because they took a trip there, or spoke to a relative or refugee from there, can add a puzzle piece to the growing database of information. Could some of it be inaccurate or intentionally misleading? Of course, but the point of the self-correcting nature of large, independent crowds is that weird "outlier" data is likely to be recognized, contradicted and thrown out.

Distributed user networks can also break down large problems, like a horde of ants. There have been suggestions that complex documents, or collections of documents, be put online for crowd analysis. If Congress is considering a 2,000 page healthcare bill with another 800 pages of amendments (which none of the members of Congress has even read in its entirety), why not put it online for a week and allow a hundred thousand people with diverse interests and backgrounds to comb through it? The crowd might find something that someone else missed--*or hid*--in it.

YouTube and social networking sites have forever changed how we discover what's going on during a crisis. During the Iranian antigovernment protests in the summer of 2009, thousands of cellphone users were able to get out pictures, video, and text messages from the scene. We now get eyewitness updates from disasters and war zones that were never possible before.

All the above are examples of the democratizing power of information technologies. George Orwell and the futurists never imagined that communications and information technologies would become this cheap and decentralized. It has forever changed the relationship between individuals and governments. Could governments shut down the networks? They can try, but the balance of power has shifted. The personal computer and the cell-phone camera have given the people eyes, ears and voices that governments must now compete with.

I keep using Surowiecki's term, "the wisdom of crowds," but there's another word for all of this: *markets.* Some of us are suspicious of that term, but that is what the wisdom of crowds really boils down to. Markets are places where ideas, information, opportunities--anything really--compete for the votes of the crowd. Those votes are cast by belief, participation, loyalty, attention, money, etc. Say ten new movies are released on a holiday weekend. Over the next week the crowd "votes" at the box office by buying tickets. That's a market. Say several candidates run for office, advocating different solutions to some political problem. On election day the voters vote. That's a market. Every day there are markets in which new products, companies, ideas, fashions, entertainments, investments and thousands of other things compete for the "votes" of the crowd.

You know what? More often than not the market gets it right. Not always, but most of the time. Let's at least say that a free market of ideas, information, or businesses is more likely to get it right than a limited number of regulators would. Those who want to restrict free markets usually believe that if we allowed a few appointed experts to make choices for us, instead of the market, we'd be better off. That raises questions for me: who are the experts? Who chooses them? On what basis do they make the choices? Who are they accountable to?

The eighteenth-century Scottish economist Adam Smith wrote the definitive book on this topic, *The Wealth of Nations.* Smith argued that if a market was broad enough and if it had enough time it would eventually come to the right decision. He said it was as if there was an "invisible hand" guiding money and opportunities to the right places. There's nothing magic about this, it's just the wisdom of crowds, like "Ask the Audience."

If markets are so wise, then how did our economy get so broken? Wasn't it free-market economic policies, without enough oversight and regulation, that allowed predatory capitalists to raid our national wealth? Don't markets lead to irrational behaviors, the madness of crowds rather than wisdom? Am I saying that we should chase the latest fashion or fad? Should we not listen to experts? If everyone jumped off a cliff, would you do it as well?

Understand that for the wisdom of the marketplace to really function, some things need to be true. There are also pitfalls that must be avoided at all costs.

Markets can be self-influencing. For them to be wise, the thousands and millions of judgements must be honest and independent and not merely repeating each other. Imagine that a new restaurant comes to town. My friends are all raving about it. I go there on Friday night and am honestly disappointed: the service is slow, the food is marginal and overpriced. On Monday someone asks me how I liked it, and with everyone around me going on about how great it is, I figure that maybe I was just there on a bad night. I suppose that my friends must know what they're talking about, and I don't want to look stupid and unhip in front of them. I say, "Yeah, sure, it was great." Maybe I go back, with my friends, the next weekend. I'm not crazy about the place, but they seem to like it and I want to be accepted by the group, so I go along. Other people do the same thing with their friends. The restaurant is packed for several months, and everyone in town assumes that it must be good because everyone else is going there. That's an example of a crowd, or market, influencing itself. It isn't functioning as independently voting individuals. This is the biggest reason markets fail. We have a tendency to *follow* the market's judgment, not *contribute to* it.

You have probably seen the Navy Blue Angels flight team; four jets that do exciting precision maneuvers at air shows. The U.S. Air Force has a similar team, the Thunderbirds. On January 21, 1982, however, all four of the Thunderbird's jets crashed while practicing at an air base in Nevada. To maintain their tight and coordinated formations, only the lead pilot on teams like the Thunderbirds or Blue Angels watches their position relative to the ground. Essentially, the lead pilot executes the maneuver. The other pilots are trained to watch the tail or wingtip of the plane next to them, which can be only inches away, to maintain their position and distance. On that day in 1982 the lead pilot was diving out of a loop maneuver into the desert floor, and was supposed to pull level at an altitude of 100 feet. For whatever reason he failed to pull out in time. The other three pilots, flying in a diamond formation with their eyes fixed on his tail or wingtip, followed him with their ordinary precision right into the ground.

In the same way, a market's judgement can lead to dramatic failure when members follow the bad decisions of a few leaders, or even just one. When the financial media reports that some celebrity investor is putting all of his money into a certain start-up company, everyone else figures that he knows something that they don't, and they follow him as precisely as those Thunderbird pilots. The same principle applies to politics, fashion, entertainment and every other venue where the wisdom of the crowd becomes the stampede of a herd.

This is how "bubble markets" form. A market stops functioning as a million independent voices, and becomes a single voice repeated a million times. Everyone is buying tech stocks and you don't want to get left behind, do you? Everyone else is flipping houses, you don't want to miss this wave, do you? More and more people "vote" with their money and the price becomes inflated way beyond the rational value of the thing everyone is buying. It lasts for a while, until the bubble bursts and everyone realizes that they bought high and now have to sell low--except for the first investor who started the bubble. He was probably the first in and the first out and made a lot of money. His success will be repeated over and over while all the rest lick their wounds.

This is one of the reasons so many have gotten sucked into multilevel marketing, including me. We listened to a limited number of people whose opinions had been repeated over and over again through advertising, sales pitches and enthusiastic conferences. The truth was that a few people had made some money early on in a business venture. Then a system had been set up to promote their success. Enthusiasm, wishful thinking and the madness (not wisdom) of crowds kicked in. The "pioneer" stories were repeated over and over again until it seemed like a vast crowd of voices all extolling the success of some business model. Like the Thunderbird pilots, the rest of us just followed the wingtips of our "upline."

Markets don't care about you. They have no emotion. They aren't benevolent or malevolent. They are just the aggregate votes of a large number of people. When there are enough of them and they are rational and independent of each other, then aggregate wisdom can be found. If they just repeat the judgment of a few leaders they become a stampede of lemmings over a cliff. Remember the ox weighing contest? What if you had been there, but instead of looking at the ox and making your own guess you wandered around the crowd asking advice from people who seemed friendly or knowledgeable (or worse, people who offered to sell you their advice). Your bid might be wildly off because you got bad advice. When Galton did his calculations the average might have been wildly off because there had been only a few genuine bids but they had been repeated repeatedly. The crowd was only wise because 800 people, most of them probably farmers familiar with oxen, had all given honest guesses without consulting each other.

There are two other important reasons that markets sometimes behave stupidly. The first is when they "vote" based on insufficient or even deceptive information. What if the people, during Galton's ox-weighing contest, had been shown some *other* ox, not the actual ox that was weighed? What if there had been something wrong with the ox, like it had a weird disease that doubled the density of its bones? The market would have been skewed because it had been *misled.* This happens far too often, and it's one reason that we do need some laws requiring that the information provided to markets is honest. If a company fudges its financial reports, investors can't fairly evaluate its stock price.

The other way markets can be skewed is when some outside force, that has no rational connection with the item being voted on, influences the votes of the crowd. For example, suppose that a new president signed a law offering tax incentives to anyone who put plastic, pink flamingos on his front lawn. Plastic flamingo sales would go through the roof, and some investors might start buying stock in flamingo factories, or even plastic suppliers. Suppose also that two years later a new congress repeals the Pink Flamingo Incentive Act. All of a sudden, it is revealed that the real demand for pink flamingo ornaments is quite small. Many people who had invested their retirement savings during the Flamingo Boom would be angry, and feel that they were misled by the market. Yet the market hadn't functioned with complete freedom, it had been influenced by non-market forces. This was one factor in the housing bubbles in the years leading up to 2008. Government programs had encouraged, or outright subsidized, the purchase of homes for people who otherwise would not have been creditworthy, thus artificially driving up values. This is happening right now with some "green technologies." When government incentives are removed many of them will collapse and a lot of people will be angry with Wall Street again, when it was government policies that built the bubble.

This is the most important paragraph in this entire chapter. After all we have learned about the wisdom of crowds and the power of markets, there is one thing above all others that we need, and each of us must take responsibility for cultivating it in our own mind and daily practice. I wish that there was a better way to say it, but I don't think there is, so here it goes: we must develop really effective "b.s." detectors. We can't be so darned gullible. We need to know, by instinct, when the crowd has become a stampede, or when the market is being manipulated. There are no set rules, no procedures, that we can come up with to protect ourselves. P.T. Barnum said: "There's a sucker born every minute," and if you're too trusting, lazy or downright stupid you *will* get screwed. No government can protect you from that. Heck, it may be the government that screws you, or the antigovernment crusaders. Either way, take a long view of market trends, get a ton of data and develop street smarts. Be shrewd or get screwed. Don't just question authority, question *everything.*

Free markets--whether of ideas, speech, entertainment, religion, political candidates, products, services or investments--can protect us from tyranny. They can expose fraud. Recently, a friend of mine was almost recruited to buy into a franchise business, but ten minutes with Google revealed it to be a shady operation (it's ironic that one of the first things they tell you at a multilevel marketing meeting is not to do any online research, and not to believe anything you read online about the company or the speakers at the meeting). Sometimes markets stumble, for a while. More often than not, over time, the wisdom of markets has brought the world more peace and prosperity than all the schemes of political experts ever have.

Generation X has been given a historic gift. The technological revolution we grew up with makes all these markets, whether conceptual or political, cultural or financial, more effective than ever before. We have a mighty weapon to defend our freedom. We need to understand these markets. We need to grasp their strengths and weaknesses and learn how to harness them to overcome the problems America faces.

Let's close this chapter with some questions. What is more likely to happen in the next twenty years as it becomes our turn to lead this country: that we will have too much freedom to speak, choose, buy and spend...or too little? If cultural, political and financial markets are restricted and regulated, who will regulate them? How? On what basis? To what end? Who will regulate the regulators? Will we be better off than if we had let the members of the crowd vote with their own participation and money?

Chapter 14
"The Wealth of the Generations"

You may not like me.

Ever since I had the idea to write this book I've been haunted by the suspicion that a lot readers might be really turned off by my story and my moralizing. Some of you might think of me as a complete hypocrite. I borrowed a lot of money, managed my affairs badly and left my creditors hanging. I'm one of the many people who contributed to the housing and credit crisis that sent the country into a recession. That would be enough for a lot of you to dislike me, but then I've had the audacity to write a book preaching about wisdom and restraint. Easy for me to say, huh? Let's be totally clear: I learned everything I've written about the hard way, by doing the opposite of what I've been encouraging us all to do in this book. It was a nightmare for everyone involved: my family, friends, business colleagues, creditors and just about everybody else who knew me or dealt with me.

Beyond disliking me, you may resent me. Yes, I went through a painful few years, but in the end we were able to use bankruptcy laws to walk away from most of our screw-ups. It's probably galling to think that outside of a house payment we're now nearly debt free while you've spent years living responsibly to pay your debts.

If it helps (and it probably doesn't) I'm sickened by what I did and I still lose sleep over it. I'm sincerely remorseful, but what can I do now? The only thing I can do is to learn from my mistakes and move forward, putting what I've learned to use in my life and the lives of others I can influence. In the first chapter I told you about my bankruptcy hearing. Throughout the book I've talked about what I learned through that process about our culture and country. I've tried to be honest (maybe too much) and as the book winds down, I'd like to share with you how my thinking and life have both changed.

I get asked, a lot, how I could have been so stupid as to do some of the things that I did. One thing I've learned about myself on this journey is that I'm easily influenced by other people; or at least I'm inclined to be. I've talked throughout the book about the seductions and myths that Generation X is susceptible to, and I'm the worst type of offender. I had affluenza, I was a child of the Society of the Spectacle and I was always looking for a shortcut. Those things inclined me to listen to anyone who I thought could help me "jump the line" and get in with the hip crowd. Back in the nineteenth century P.T. Barnum said, "There's a sucker born every minute," because there have always been bad people who are ready and willing to take advantage of suckers like me. Whenever I got myself into a jam, I would blame it on the people around me: the bankers who encouraged me to sign, my business partners who talked me into something, the "friends" who told me I had nothing to worry about. A few years ago, as my world was crashing, I was whining to a friend about all the people who had led me astray. He interrupted, and told me that I was like the kid in high school who lets potheads ride in his car and then one day gets pulled over for speeding. The cop finds a bag of weed in the back seat and the kid always whines, *"But it's not mine officer! It belongs to a friend!"* I've had to learn to stop blaming the strangers who sold me the magic beans. More than that, I've had to learn to stop hanging around with people like that and letting them be an influence in my life.

We all need to do that. We can't blame the politicians or the media or the celebrities or the advertisers. It's not Joe Camel's fault our kids smoke, Ronald McDonald's fault we eat too much fat, Tony the Tiger's fault we eat too much sugar or the fault of "predatory lenders" that we maxed out our Visa cards and bought houses we couldn't afford. Generation X doesn't have a reputation for standing up and taking responsibility, but that's exactly what we're going to have to do as it becomes our turn to lead America.

How do we tell the bad influences from the good ones? Who are the *trustworthy* politicians, financial advisors and authors? Who are the ones we should run away from? It's hard to articulate the difference, except in hindsight. Over time we can develop instincts. It reminds me of what Justice Potter Stewart said in a famous Supreme Court opinion, trying to define pornography: "I know it when I see it."

One thing that I have learned about *un*trustworthy influences and sources is that they never want us to look backward and learn from the past. So I've put this little rule in place for my life going forward: *always look backwards.*

I mentioned my Grandfather earlier in this book, the one with the boats. A couple years ago we lost him after he contracted a hospital staph infection following successful heart surgery. It was by far, the worst day of my life. My uncle died later that same day as a result of the small plane crash I mentioned in an earlier chapter. In total, my wife and I attended 5 funerals of family members in about an 18-month period in the middle of our financial collapse, but Grandpa was by far the hardest for me.

We got the phone call a little after 6 a.m., telling us that he had died. I went downstairs and sat at the piano (which a few months later I had to sell to keep us in a home with food). The piano has always been an emotional release for me, way better than the black couch. I found myself playing the old gospel hymn "It is Well With my Soul." But all wasn't well with my soul. Not just because Grandpa was gone, but also because Grandpa never got to see me do something well. I don't think he ever really knew all the details of my woes. He may have even been flattered that I bought a boat early in adulthood; after all it was Grandpa who took me boating, skiing, and fishing on his boats. I would have wanted his approval not just because he was my Grandpa but because he represented what many would argue was that last great generation, possibly the greatest.

He was a hero to me, a man worth modeling my life after. His entire generation, the WWII generation, were heroes. Children of the

Great Depression, they fought a great war against a great evil. They returned and launched the Great Abundance: more than fifty years of unprecedented economic and technological expansion. In my Grandpa's case, he left shortly after marrying my Grandma and didn't return home for four years. Today, we wouldn't think of sending a soldier oversees for four straight years. Can you imagine the mothers picketing on the steps of the White House while their baby boys risked their lives if we did that today? My Grandma's generation of women were too busy running factories that had been converted from making cars to making tanks to worry about picketing in Washington. My Grandpa would write my Grandma letters and the first letter of each paragraph would spell out the name of the South Pacific island he was on. With no satellite phones or email, just paper and a pen, no television or Internet coverage, back home they had to wait to find out what was happening by reading about it days, or sometimes weeks, later in a newspaper.

My wife also had a Grandpa who fought. Many, maybe even most of us did. I'm grateful and honored to have known him as well before we lost him a few years ago. He was a member of the Dutch Underground in the Netherlands, hiding Jews from the Nazis. At one point a friend of his joined the Nazi army and betrayed him at his front door by shooting him through the chest. He survived and moved his family with four children to America, enduring nine days of rough ocean and the seasickness that came with it. Upon arrival they settled into a small farm in Fennville, MI where they often had little or no food. They would tell stories of praying at the table for food and then going to the mailbox to find a loaf of bread. They were immigrants who made the effort to learn English, the language of their new country. Until the day he died, his mere presence in a room was prominent. Without words he earned respect because of who he was and what he had done. If you asked, he'd show you the scar in his chest where the bullet entered, and the scar on his back where it exited.

As I write this, the History Channel has been airing a show called WWII in HD (apparently they do still broadcast actual history programs from time to time). It's an amazing show; buy it on DVD if you can. There are no recreated scenes; only actual WWII footage reformatted in HD. Our generation is absolutely clueless as to what it means to pay the kind of price that our grandparents did. We can't really comprehend what it means to struggle, much less suffer. We think a recession sucks because we lose our jobs and custom homes. Not having health insurance is a crisis to us. Those things are bad, but to put it into perspective, imagine having to abandon your sinking battleship and then drifting with your few surviving shipmates in the middle of the Pacific Ocean. Then imagine watching one of your fellow survivors have a leg bitten off by a shark and having to make the decision to offer him up to the other sharks to save the rest of your lives. Of course that pales in comparison to not having prescription coverage for our Viagra and Prozac.

It's not just that they fought a horrible war, it was their willingness to do it. They understood the idea of responsibility. They grew up in the Depression and learned what has actual value, like food and shelter and work and church (even without the movie screens and electric guitars). They valued and worked for things that have stood the test of time and proven worthwhile. They came back from war and accepted responsibility for building a better America and a better world for their kids and grandkids. They learned to be content with smaller houses, even though their families were bigger. Grandma still lives in the same house Grandpa built sixty years ago, and there's no place I'd rather go for the family Christmas party.

Part of what made that generation great was that they didn't depend on marketers, pollsters, and spin doctors to tell them what had value. Throughout the Depression, World War II and the post-war years, they mostly pulled together and did the right thing. They didn't claim personal rights as an excuse not to defend the well-being of the nation as a whole.

I've had several conversations with people during the writing of this book about the idea of "Value versus Values." People challenge my definition of value and ask how I can support it. I'm not a philosopher, but like Justice Stewart's definition of pornography, I think I know it when I see it. At least I do now. If you don't, then you just don't get it.

Our grandparents understood that it was better to own a 1,200 square-foot home than to heavily finance a 4,000 square-foot McMansion. They figured that it was better to save money than to owe it. When they built the Interstate highways, they paid for them and didn't just kick the deficit can down the road to their kids, even though their children's generation, the baby boomers, was large enough to have borne it. By contrast, the boomers are kicking *$10 trillion* of debt to us, a generation 58% their size. Now we're on track to do something even worse to our kids. We should at least extend to them the courtesy of teaching them Chinese if this is going to continue so that they can talk to their bankers. The WWII generation was the Greatest Generation because no one had to tell them what to do, they just did it.

Thanks to our grandparents, we grew up in one of the most prosperous eras in the history of the world. We didn't have to experience what they did and therefore didn't learn first hand what they learned. We are an *intelligent* generation (again thanks to our grandparents), but they were *wise.* We play the role of victim really well. We are victims, probably to a greater extent than most generations. We are victims of our own ignorance *and* our own intelligence. We are victims of our own shortsightedness *and* our farsightedness. Farsighted in the sense that we easily look forward to amazing futures. We make creative movies about the distant future, but are shortsighted in our ability to look backwards beyond our own childhoods. Growing up in the bubble has caused us to misplace and misunderstand the bigger reality around us.

There really is nothing new under the sun. I am not the first to file bankruptcy and I won't be the last. We are not the first generation to have to take the reins of the country in a recession. The more important question is: will we be wise enough to stop this process of putting Band Aids on dinosaurs to protect our perfect little world? Will we stop and decide to change? Dare I say to *grow up?*

I find it ironic that we elected a president whose campaign was built on the word "change." He has no control over that, because change is inevitable. I think we elected him because we hoped he would make hard choices for us so that we wouldn't have to. What we really want is someone to pull some sort of magical policy rabbit out of a hat that will prevent the wave of change that's coming over us. We don't want to give up our values, our stuff or our comfortable bubble. We don't want to change. If we make this Washington's problem then we won't have to deal with it. Think again. Washington? Really? Do you really want Washington handling our problems? Do I have to tell you why that's a bad idea or does that fit into the "you'll-know-it's-a-bad-idea-when-you-see-it" category?

My co-author Greg teaches a class on the Law of Gravity. Applied to life (not just apples falling from a tree), he says that there are irresistible forces in history that pull everything back down toward certain natural states, or back to "earth" if you will. Like it or not, America is coming back to Earth. We must look backwards to realize the type of changes that we have to make if this new, non-virtual, reality is going to be good for us and our children. I'm not talking about reverting to horse-drawn carriages or getting rid of our cell phones and magic boxes that entertain and sell us stuff. I'm talking about relearning the idea of responsibility that got lost as the WWII generation grew older and a generation many times larger started taking over.

You know what's interesting about that greatest generation? Despite losing hundreds of thousands of their friends and family at war, despite spending their childhoods in bread lines, despite hard physical labor building roads and houses, despite living in small homes, they were mostly then, and still are, happy. They call those days the good old days. They don't have our stress, even though they had more cause. On second thought, perhaps that's not entirely accurate. They are stressed about us.

Today, my wife and I don't have a new car or a car loan, even though the TV tells us to. We don't have credit cards (not like anyone would give us one anyway) and we probably never will. I read books now, which would have been hard for me to imagine a few years ago. I have a mentor and we have good, solid friendships with no hidden agendas. We hang out with people who don't do bad or stupid things, or influence us to. We don't buy "stuff" just to have it anymore, and we even look for the sale items at the grocery store. The biggest change is this: We really just don't value the valueless things that we used to care so much about. Stuff, material wealth, worldly success, and affluenza just don't matter like they used to. Sure, I won't deny it: I'd love to have a boat again. There's nothing wrong with having a boat or anything like that, as long as it doesn't compromise good financial stewardship and good sense. We eliminated the influences that had convinced us that stuff like boats made us better. They don't.

The hardest part of writing this book hasn't really been worrying about what most readers might think. I've been criticized, humiliated and humbled so much over the last few years that nothing really gets to me anymore. What's really bothered me is wondering what my Grandpa would have thought.

He gave me an incredible example and I ignored it. Worse, I was bored by it. Maybe, deep down inside I secretly despised it a little because it would have required actual work. All of us still have an opportunity to sit with these great men and women and gain some actual wisdom that no one else can give us. There are countless other examples from around the world throughout thousands of years of history that we have access to as well. Even though I'm pretty critical of the baby boomers, you'll find some wisdom there as well. I'm one of the few Gen Xer's who has great parents that stayed married and still get along. There is wisdom in that. I can't imagine how my wife and I would have gotten through our struggles, let alone kept our own marriage together, without our parents.

We need to stop looking for some great new philosopher or president or celebrity to bring us some miracle solution, and start looking backwards. Our cleverness won't solve our problems, we need to find some wisdom as well.

The wealth of the generations is not the material legacy. In my family it isn't the boats, cars or inheritance my grandparents will leave behind. Perhaps we can learn not to just chase money, but to pursue a genuine wealth and security. The wealth of the generations is wisdom that can only come from experience, not just our own, but that of our forebears.

Conclusion
"It's Our Turn"

I wish that all we had to do was blow up a Death Star.

Of course I can't speak for every member of my generation, but I was raised on *Star Wars* and so I, for one, was ready for *that.* If the challenges of the next ten or twenty years were that obvious (a big, mechanical moon) with a single-point-of-failure design flaw (a main reactor exhaust port) and we could score a "direct hit" by just "trusting our feelings"--well, you know, I'm gonna guess that we could probably get that done.

After 9/11 a lot of us assumed that we could just unleash our muscle and money (the most powerful military the world has ever known, funded by the most powerful economy in history) and fix the problem. The problem turned out to be more complicated than that. We haven't caught Osama bin Laden, and while we did prevent another attack on our homeland, the forces that brought the Twin Towers down are still out there, still threatening to do us harm.

I feel stupid saying this now, but perhaps *Star Wars* and the rest of our pop culture wasn't the best possible preparation for the real world. Maybe we like to imagine solutions to things like possible asteroid strikes and global warming because they fit our script for how the world is supposed to work: a big, evil, external threat that can be defeated with brains and technology.

The real-world problems that Generation X will have to lead through are not easily understood, much less solved. No clever "viral marketing" campaign, no benefit concert or government research effort like the Apollo space program can fix them. Do you know why?

Because *we* are the problem.

It's us, the unwashed masses of America, that create and perpetuate all of our dilemmas. Like the people of Farnham village in 1348, enough of us are carrying a disease, spreading it around to each other, that none of us ever gets better. It's killing us. We, the people, must change. No one else can or should do it for us.

As we all know, the first step to solving a problem is to acknowledge that we have it. For starters, we need to admit that we have a dysfunctional relationship with money. At every level of society--individuals, families, companies, government--we are addicted to spending more than we have, often on things we don't need. We've talked about the why and the how, but the bottom line is that Generation X's nemesis will be a *Debt* Star instead of a Death Star. It will not be blown up with a direct hit, guided by our feelings. It will require deep, real, lasting and courageous change in America.

Some debt is inevitable and tolerable in a capitalist economy, especially a growing economy. Capital markets have created the modern world, and few of us really want to live in the undeveloped countries, which almost by definition are those that never developed capital markets or mechanisms. America in 2009 has a culture and system that keeps kicking our can of debt down the road for the next generation to pay off. We hope that we can grow the economy out of it. We're running out of road, and we can't kick this can any further. Somehow in the next ten or twenty years we are going to have to finally deal with our staggering private and public debts.

I can't help remembering Princess Leia pleading in that hologram, "Help me, Obi-Wan Kenobi, you're my only hope!" Again, if it could only be that simple: we send out a call for help and some hero swoops in and makes America solvent again. As I've said throughout this book, I'm convinced that the only real hope that we have is to rediscover the concept of *value.* We must learn to recognize and act on genuine value in business, family, politics, religion, entertainment, and all other areas of life. If we will become value-driven we will treat each other better, spend our money more carefully, use our time more wisely, and hold our leaders more accountable. It will break our death spiral of spending and borrowing.

Each one of us is going to have to do this. We can't expect the government to do it, for two reasons. First, because the habit of passing on to others what we don't have the discipline to do ourselves is exactly what got us into this mess in the first place. Second, because the government *can't* do it, it's broke. The phrase "full faith and credit of the United States" used to be as safe a bet as is possible in this world, but we've become collectively what too many of us are individually: in over our heads, living paycheck to paycheck. We're each going to have to clean up our mess, and if we do, only then do we have a chance to climb out of the collective hole we've dug ourselves into.

In 2008 we voted for "change," whatever that meant. We have to do more than *vote* for change, we have to *actually change.* Not change each other, but change ourselves. We need new perspectives, attitudes and lifestyles, and unless we start soon it will be too late. My hope is that our generation's legacy will be one of making lasting changes that free America to grow into a new century of peace and prosperity. I hear the phrase all too often: "our kids are screwed." I refuse to accept that.

What, exactly, must we change? Well, if most of us just began, starting today, to implement the following twelve action items (A Twelve Step Program for Generation X), we will be able to adapt to whatever the twenty-first century throws at us.

1. ***Recognize the Power of the Media/Advertising Complex In Our Lives.*** The baby boomers were terrified of the "Military Industrial Complex." They became paranoid about it, catching glimpses of it everywhere and believing it was the invisible hand that pulled all the levers in our society. I don't want us to swap out our parents' paranoia for a new one, but I think that we ought to recognize that the media/advertising/entertainment industries (which are all huge conglomerates at this point) have far more influence on

our lives at this point than companies that make fighter jets. I would argue that they are more insidious than the military-industrial companies ever were because they shape the worldview and steer the choices of our children. Let's be honest: who wields more power over the lives of our teenagers, Sony Entertainment or Northrup-Grumman? It's important that we remain skeptical of not only what we see/hear/read, but of the belief systems and motives of the entertainers and advertisers that craft our perceptions of the world around us.

2. ***Read.*** When we were kids, people still learned things by reading books. Baby boomers like Bill Gates and Steve Jobs may have given the world the personal computer, but we gave it blogs, Facebook and YouTube. Those things aren't necessarily bad, but our knowledge of the world has become self-catered: our window on the world is the bookmarked pages in our web browser. And our window is getting smaller: 140 characters on Twitter, a two-inch square on our smart phone. Books, on the other hand, aren't just old technology, they're a different *type* of communication. We may roll our eyes at a twenty-page chapter, but some ideas take twenty pages to explore. We're so busy texting each other that we've lost the art of conversation. Books are a conversation, a way of really sharing stories, cultures, history, and language. Some people say that books will go the way of the buggy whip. If so, then we're becoming a global village instantly sharing trivial information. Why do we say that we don't have time to read? Do we really have less time than people did thirty years ago? Why? Is it because reading would cut into our TV, Facebook, and video

games? I'm not saying that we shouldn't use all these great tools, but we'd be a healthier and happier world if we shut off the electronics sometimes and read a book about people, places and things that we knew nothing about.

3. ***Live Within Our Means.*** Even better, live *below* our means. If we become a nation of savers, if we break the vicious cycle of spend and borrow, we will change America more powerfully than any boatload of new government programs (funded with more borrowed money) ever could. This one thing would be the key to improving our lives in so many other ways. Right now, even in a recession, America and Americans have a lot of income, but we don't have much wealth left because it's all been mortgaged. If we simply spent less than we earned, we'd start accumulating wealth again, and be able to give again. Bam. Just like that.

4. ***Invest in Relationships and Protect That Investment.*** It's a cliché to say that people should mean more to us than things, but it's true. We have no idea what the next twenty years will bring. Our standard of living could go up or down, the earth could get warmer or colder, Skynet could become self-aware and unleash the terminators on us. Regardless of our circumstances, we can face life with loved ones or without them. Friendship, kindness, love, loyalty...these things are free. Difficult times don't test love, they reveal it. The baby boomers sang songs and wrote books about it, but they were the original "me generation" and their legacy has been narcissism. We grew up in the wake of their self-

centeredness, and Generation X has a reputation for being cynical and incapable of deep attachments. If we resolve that our legacy will be one of investing deeply in people and then protecting that investment with selflessness and loyalty, we will leave America a better place than we found it.

5. ***Value Value.*** The first is a verb, the second is a direct object: we must *place value* on things that are *valuable.* We spent an entire chapter talking about the difference between values (what's important to me) and value (what's important to all of us). All our arguments about values are really just shoving matches about our personal priorities. We need to get past that and build our lives around discovering and acting upon the real, intrinsic worth of things. Not only would we leave behind an ethically and socially better country, we would pop bubble markets before they got started. We wouldn't as easily catch the mass hysteria that causes us to trample over each other in a race to buy up overpriced stocks, real estate or Beanie Babies. The proper response to someone who tells you it's *clever* to take out a $400,000 no-doc mortgage with nothing down and a $50,000 income, and then to leverage that to buy two more houses to flip (because if you don't you'll get left behind!) is, *"Do you take me for a fool?"* Of course, their response would probably be, "Yes." In which case you happily stay behind the stampeding herd so that when the bubble bursts you'll be living in a house that's properly valued. If Generation X resolved to buy things based on their real value and gave real value when we sold our labor or products, we will be a *valuable* generation.

6. ***Love Work.*** We have deeply conflicted attitudes toward work in our culture. We have a holiday called "Labor Day" on which we don't work. Isn't that something like having a national "Sports Day" on which there are no scheduled athletic events and everyone is supposed to refrain from playing any spontaneous pickup games? Maybe on Labor Day we should all work for free, to celebrate the value of work? I know: it's a crazy, stupid idea. Still, we need to return to valuing work, not just as a means to an end (get money), but as something valuable and beautiful in itself. It's one of the things that separates us from the animals. Animals do what they have to do to eat, but humans invent wheels, build cities, paint frescos on the walls of cathedrals, manufacture potato chips and send rocket ships into space. Work is the purposeful channeling of human intellect, creativity and ambition. I think that it's fair to say that every tangible value that we can point to in human society is the byproduct of work. Other countries were built on forced labor, feudalism and slavery. Those are sad chapters in American history as well, but no other great nation has been as much the result of its citizens valuing and loving work as the United States. Work was an ideal, and it was self-given: you can ask someone else to give you a job, but only you can make yourself work. We're all obsessed with how the government is going to "create jobs," but maybe if Americans were more focused on creating work for themselves--whatever form that took--the job creation would follow in its wake.

7. ***Go Outside.*** Following up on my previous point, how much healthier and happier would we be if we just turned off the

electronics sometimes and went for a walk? Without the iPod. I know, now I just sound crazy again, but I'm serious. Some of us can still remember our parents chasing us outside to play, back before electronics hypnotized all of us. What if we were a little bit less plugged in? I'm sure that we'd be physically and emotionally healthier and might learn the names of the people who live next door. To stay in touch with reality we need to unplug from the Matrix sometimes and just go to the park and throw a Frisbee around or something. Generation X invented the virtual world, and it's up to us to recognize the limits of what we've created.

8. ***Pursue Global Policies that Have Been Proven to Work.*** Too much of our view of the world is rooted in fantasy or ideology. We believe what we want to believe about international affairs, but it doesn't always match up with reality. We all do it: conservatives and liberals, isolationists and globalists. Our fantasies and ideologies are based in all sorts of things. Religion, upbringing, what we were taught in school, what we've seen in the movies, what we've read, what some politician or celebrity said, or what we observed on some vacation or college, study-abroad trip. We take all these inputs, mix them with our prejudices and biases, filter them through our worldviews and self-interests and often attach them to someone's agenda. This is the way we form our ideas about things in America as well, but the difference is that it's harder to verify our beliefs about things on the other side of the globe. What do you or I *really* know about Christianity in China, about terrorist-sympathizers in Waziristan, about the economics of the middle class in Mumbai, about debt in Africa, about

glaciers in Greenland or the refugee camps in Darfur? Not much. We have lots of opinions, and we're always signing on to advocate some action: fight a war here, impose a carbon tax there, restrict imports somewhere else, boycott somebody in protest over something. Most of us have absolutely no idea what the heck we're talking about (including me), but we don't let that stop us from advocating, protesting, bloviating, blogging or just buying a T-shirt to show our concern and send a dollar to some organization somewhere that's going to do something about it sometime. If we were talking about affairs in our city or state we'd see through this nonsense, because we can observe the problems first hand and demand that any solutions make things better in the real world. So here's my modest proposal for Generation X: let's demand that any global causes we advocate for produce real results. I don't care if you're on the left or the right, the principle of demonstrated results and accountability is bipartisan. Let's demand that the leaders of governments and NGO's (non-governmental organizations) stick with proven solutions, or invent new ones directly based on models that have proved effective. And when they want to try something new, make them accountable for results. We've spent enough blood and treasure on schemes to end all sorts of real and imagined problems around the globe. Most of it has been wasted, and in many cases made the problems worse. I could fill another book with examples. If this book sells, maybe I will.

9. ***Do Business the Right Way.*** Calvin Coolidge isn't one of our better-known presidents, but he coined a phrase that's become

iconic: "The business of America is business." That quote has come under withering fire for defending crass and greedy free-market policies. I was curious, so I looked it up. I found that Coolidge said that in a speech to the American Society of Newspaper Editors, in Washington D.C., on January 17, 1925. It's an excellent speech. The famous quote is part of a larger paragraph in which he argues that the press in America (today we'd say the media) needs to understand how the business world works, because it is the business world that not only keeps most Americans occupied but feeds, clothes and houses them as well. Business activity is also the only thing that generates the taxes that feed the government, and so Coolidge argues that the media had better understand how the system works so that they don't advocate stupid policies that kill the goose laying the golden eggs. Here's the excerpt:

> *"...a press which maintains an intimate touch with the business currents of the nation, is likely to be more reliable than it would be if it were a stranger to these influences. After all, the chief business of the American people is business. They are profoundly concerned with producing, buying, selling, investing and prospering in the world. I am strongly of the opinion that the great majority of people will always find these are moving impulses of our life... It is only when they cease production, when accumulation stops, that an irreparable decay begins. Wealth is the product of industry, ambition, character and untiring effort. In all experience, the accumulation of wealth means the multiplication of schools,*

> *the increase of knowledge, the dissemination of intelligence, the encouragement of science, the broadening of outlook, the expansion of liberties, the widening of culture. Of course, the accumulation of wealth cannot be justified as the chief end of existence. But we are compelled to recognize it as a means to well nigh every desirable achievement. So long as wealth is made the means and not the end, we need not greatly fear it."*

Generation X needs to restore a right relationship between Americans and America's business. No more vaporware. No more Debt Star. No more government know-it-alls who think they are smarter than the free market and making decisions for all of us. On the other hand, no more out-of-scale, too-big-to-fail investment schemes or gigantic and lethargic companies that need bail outs, either. While we're at it, no more affluenza: being busy with business doesn't have to make us gluttons for consumer excess. We can be productive and frugal. Productivity and frugality is a potent combination that leads to genuine wealth, not just cash flow trickling through our fingers. From genuine wealth comes the opportunity for sincere and lasting generosity and philanthropy. When Americans have been rich, we have given through our communities, churches, colleges, hospitals and thousands of other ways. We've been the most generous and philanthropic society in history. Now we're broke, and instead of generosity we are forced to give to a bloated government, aided by a media which apparently thinks that we really do have magic beans and a goose that lays golden eggs. We need to figure this out, and fast, or America will be in Chapter Seven with a fill-in attorney.

10. ***Support and Defend the Constitution Against All Enemies, Foreign and Domestic.*** That's the oath of office that the president and other members of the federal government, including the armed forces, take. Here's an idea: let's *all* take that oath. The Constitution is not a magic document, but it is the basis of our republic and the *only* thing that gives our government any right to exist, much less to act. There's a story about the Constitutional Convention, in which founding fathers drafted the articles of government, that captures the spirit of that enterprise. Supposedly, a woman asked Ben Franklin what form of government they had given us. He responded, "A republic, ma'am, if you can keep it." A republic is not a direct democracy. In practice direct democracy can become a mob. A republic is and was a representative democracy that entrusts a government with limited powers to act according to defined principles. Franklin recognized, as did all the authors of the Constitution, that keeping a republic functioning required diligence and vigilance. It required the government to exercise restraint, to "color inside the lines" by staying within its mandated jurisdiction and remaining faithful to the ideals of the republic. It required a vigorous electorate to hold government accountable. Generation X is coming of age and coming to the realization that the entire political class in America has failed to keep the republic. The government acts without regard to the Constitution, which is its only basis for existence. The ideals of restraint and accountability have been corrupted. We all should

vow, like federal officials, to support and defend the Constitution against all its enemies, whether they be foreign or right here at home. We need to act on that as vigorously as we can without undermining the Constitution or the principles of the republic ourselves in our defense of it. I wonder if that might involve nonviolent civil disobedience in the years to come. That's how the Civil Rights Movement did it. What other rights are we prepared to defend with nonviolent civil disobedience?

11. ***Leave a Generational Legacy.*** It's hard to write your own obituary, and it's perhaps morbid as well. It can be a worthwhile exercise: what will people remember about me? Here's something even more interesting: what will Generation X be remembered for? The Jazz Age generation of the 1920s gave us the Great Depression. The Great Depression and World War II gave us the Greatest Generation and the Great Abundance of the postwar world. The baby boomers gave us Rock and Roll, the Information Age and the Debt Star. What will Generation X leave to Generation Y? This isn't an academic question, it's being decided *right now.* How we live, what we do, and the decisions we make over the next few years will determine our generational legacy. Will we go down in history as the generation that lost the family farm, crying: "But it was in trouble when we inherited it!" as the Chinese bankers carry away grandma's china (ironic, I know). Will we be the generation that overcame problems and extended peace and prosperity in the world? Every move we make and every vote we take right now is contributing to one of those two legacies.

12. ***Ask The Most Important Question: Really?*** We have a reputation for being cynical, but I think we're just gullible. The World War II generation felt a sense of duty to their country. The baby boomers demanded and got what they wanted. We've just bought everything that's been sold to us. We're the most consumerist generation in history because we were the first to grow up completely saturated by media messaging. Almost every waking moment, from childhood, we've been sold brands and bands. Bands have become brands and brands sponsor bands. We've literally viewed millions of advertisements. We grew up in shopping malls and now clothes without a visible logo seem weird to us. Heck, some of our fondest memories occurred in malls, relaxing in a soothing bath of branding and messaging. Our own kids learned to recognize fast food logos before they could read. Generation X can make America a better place if we lead in substance, not in style. That's hard for us, because while we like to think that we're savvy about branding and messaging, the truth is that we just value it more than any generation ever did. We're hardwired to respond to it. We need to be able to look at someone trying to sell us something (Product or philosophy) and not *just* say, "Really? Is that the best *pitch* you can make?" but "Really? Is that *true?* Is that *verifiable?* Is that *worthwhile?*" My friend Eric told me that he and a friend determined that, "*Really?*" is the most profound question a human can ask; I tend to agree. If we can't become healthy skeptics we'll keep buying products, politicians and policies based on the strength of their *presentations.*

Ultimately, we risk becoming a generation of victims, manipulated and sold to all our lives.

We began this book by talking about the young men and women of Farnham village in 1348. They thought that when it was their turn to become the leaders of their community, the challenges they would face would be the ones that they grew up with. They couldn't foresee that by 1350 their world would be a very different kind of place. They had to solve problems that they never expected, with skills they had never developed up to that point. By the end of the 1350s everyone had been affected, and some found ways to prosper and improve their lives in the new social and economic order.

The task of each generation is to play the hand it is dealt, and hopefully to hand our kids a better world than was handed to us. That's the way life works. So what will we do over the next ten or twenty years as we step into positions of leadership? Will we develop the habits of heart and behavior that improve our lives and communities? If enough of us do, then when we retire we'll leave a better America for Generations who take our place.

About the Author

Rob Stam lives in Holland, Michigan with his wife and son. He frequently speaks to groups about discovering the difference between success and failure in business and life. Through his consulting business, The Big Red Group, he helps entrepreneurs figure out how to grow their business while avoiding the mistakes he made. He is working on another book on that topic.

You can learn more, arrange for him to speak to your group or contact him by visiting *www.robstam.com.*

About the Co-Author

Greg Smith is a writer, teacher and designer. He lives with his family in Holland, Michigan, and is senior partner in Black Lake Studio/Press. You can contact him by visiting *www.blacklakestudio.com.*

www.ingramcontent.com/pod-product-compliance
Lightning Source LLC
LaVergne TN
LVHW090937080826
845145LV00003B/777

* 9 7 8 0 9 8 2 4 4 4 6 0 3 *